John Newmeir

Enjoy!
08/9/2018

MANSHIP'S MILLION DOLLARS OF RARE SOUL

The exceptional records displayed within these pages were sourced from some of the finest soul 45 collections in the world.

John Manship would especially like to thank Martin Barnfather (Soul Sam), Mick Heffernan, John Ridley, Kenny Burrell, Carl Willinghan, Richard Watt, Rick Nahm, Carl Fortnum, Ginger Taylor, Mark Dobson, Adrian Potts, Rico Tee, George Hunt, and John Weston for allowing me access to their most prized 45s.

Value
range $850 to $30,000

$

Be patient this record will become available at some time but be prepared for competition and pay a high 3 figure or even low 4 figure sum to acquire it.

$$

Seldom seen for sale will most certainly reach a low 4 figure amount at auction.

$$$

A rare 45 and considered a fine example of rare soul music expect serious competition to acquire a copy

$$$$

The ultimate in rare soul collecting expect to pay whatever it takes to own it

$$$$$

Just a dream...

Rarity

Many copies known to exist but very seldom seen for sale. All copies safely filed in the world's finest Soul collections, rarity being created by the collectors' reluctance to sell.

Estimated less than 150 copies known worldwide

Estimated less than 50 copies known worldwide

Estimated less than 25 copies known worldwide

Maybe less than 10 copies known worldwide, some as little as 2 or even one copy in rare soul collections.

Quality

Value and desirability is based more on the rarity of the disc than the attraction of the music quality.

A good rare record but pales in comparison with some of the other discs displayed within these pages.

Considered a superb example of rare soul music a must acquire for all rare soul collectors.

Considered a soul record of the finest quality, revered as much for it's music as for it's rarity, highly sought after.

Considered musically as a faultless example of the finest rare soul music ever made, perfect!

highlighters band
the funky 16 corners pt.1

value $$ rarity ♦♦♦♦   quality ★★★★★

james bell & the highlighters band
the love of my girl

value $$ rarity ♦♦♦♦   quality ★★★

yum yums
gonna be a big thing

value $$ rarity ♦♦   quality ★★★★

trends
thanks for a little lovin`

value $$ rarity ♦♦♦♦   quality ★★★★

honey and the bees
two can play the same game

value	rarity	quality
$$	◆◆◆◆	★★★★

honey and the bees
be yourself

value	rarity	quality
$$	◆◆◆◆	★★★★

conquistadors
can't stop loving you

value	rarity	quality
$	◆◆	★★★★

embers
you can lump it

value	rarity	quality
$	◆◆	★★★

joe hicks
i gotta be free

value: $$
rarity: ♦♦♦
quality: ★★★★

larry wright
sweet, sweet kisses

value: $$$
rarity: ♦♦♦♦
quality: ★★★★

vondells
hey girl you've changed

value: $$$
rarity: ♦♦♦
quality: ★★★★★

martells
where can my baby be

value: $$
rarity: ♦♦♦
quality: ★★★★

hal tiore
darling i'm sorry

value	rarity	quality
$$	◆◆◆◆◆	★★★★

jimmy wallace
i'll be back

value	rarity	quality
$$	◆◆	★★★★

brown bombers & soul partners
wait for me

value	rarity	quality
$	◆◆◆	★★★★

johnny rodgers
make a change

value	rarity	quality
$$$	◆◆◆◆	★★★★

morris chestnut
too darn soulful

value rarity quality
$$ ♦♦♦   ★★★★★

lou ragland
i travel alone

value rarity quality
$$ ♦♦♦   ★★★★★

james wesley smith
talkin' 'bout women

value rarity quality
$$ ♦♦♦   ★★★

james phelps
the look on your face

value rarity quality
$$ ♦♦♦   ★★★★

billy floyd
my oh my

value | rarity | quality
$ | ♦♦ | ★★★★

kenny gamble
the jokes on you

value | rarity | quality
$$ | ♦♦♦ | ★★★★★

temptones
girl i love you

value | rarity | quality
$ | ♦♦ | ★★★★

kenny hamber
anything you want

value | rarity | quality
$ | ♦♦ | ★★★★

dyke and the blazers
funky broadway - part I

value	rarity	quality
$	♦♦♦♦	★★★

traditions
on fire

value	rarity	quality
$$$	♦♦♦♦♦	★★★★

ernie johnson
i can't stop the pain

value	rarity	quality
$$	♦♦♦♦	★★★★

eddie campbell
contagious love

value	rarity	quality
$$	♦♦♦♦	★★★

eddie parker
love you baby

value	rarity	quality
$	♦♦♦♦	★★★★★

linda and the pretenders
believe me

value	rarity	quality
$	♦♦♦♦	★★★

mary wheeler and the knights
i feel in my heart

value	rarity	quality
$$	♦♦♦	★★★★

donna colman
your loves too strong

value	rarity	quality
$	♦♦	★★★★★

eddie parker
i'm gone

value	rarity	quality
$$$$	♦♦♦♦	★★★★★

othello robertson
so in luv

value	rarity	quality
$	♦♦♦	★★★

inticers
since you left

value	rarity	quality
$$$$	♦♦♦♦♦	★★★★★

bad weather inc.
i never never knew

value	rarity	quality
$	♦♦♦	★★★

william cummings
make my love a hurting thing

value	rarity	quality
$$	♦♦♦♦	★★★★

brothers gilmore
i feel a song

value	rarity	quality
$$	♦♦♦	★★★★

don hysong
soul searcher

value	rarity	quality
$$$	♦♦♦♦	★★★★

mark iv's
the tide has turned

value	rarity	quality
$	♦♦	★★★

gallahads
i've got to find a way

value: $$
rarity: ♦♦♦
quality: ★★★

bernie williams
ever again

value: $$$
rarity: ♦♦♦
quality: ★★★★★

jim gilstrap
run, run, run

value: $$
rarity: ♦♦♦♦
quality: ★★★

tempos
render my service

value: $$$
rarity: ♦♦♦♦♦
quality: ★★★★★

esther harris
scarlet moon

value	rarity	quality
$$	♦♦♦♦	★★★

gloria & the t-aira's
i'm satisfied

value	rarity	quality
$$	♦♦	★★★★

tony daniels
i won't cry

value	rarity	quality
$$$	♦♦♦♦	★★★

oliver joy
keep love growing

value	rarity	quality
$	♦♦♦	★★★

bob & fred
i'll be on my way

value	rarity	quality
$$$	♦♦♦	★★★★

grand prix's
i see her pretty face

value	rarity	quality
$	♦♦♦	★★★

johnny mae mathews
i have no choice

value	rarity	quality
$$	♦♦♦	★★★★★

delois eaiy
don't be afraid

value	rarity	quality
$	♦♦♦♦	★★★

startones
lovin' you baby

value	rarity	quality
$	♦♦	★★★

soul set
will you ever learn

value	rarity	quality
$$	♦♦♦	★★★

trace of smoke
treasure mind

value	rarity	quality
$$$	♦♦♦♦	★★★★

eddie whitehead
just your fool

value	rarity	quality
$$$	♦♦♦♦	★★★★

informers
baby, set me free

value: $$
rarity: ♦♦♦
quality: ★★★★

ralph "soul" jackson
set me free

value: $
rarity: ♦
quality: ★★★

benny latimore
rain from the sky

value: $
rarity: ♦♦♦
quality: ★★★★

herby brown
one more broken heart

value: $$$
rarity: ♦♦♦♦
quality: ★★★★

idle few
people that's why

value	rarity	quality
$	♦♦♦♦	★★★★

charles brandy
i can't get enough of you

value	rarity	quality
$$$	♦♦♦♦♦	★★★★

ernest baker
alone again

value	rarity	quality
$	♦♦	★★★★

arin demain
silent treatment

value	rarity	quality
$$	♦♦♦	★★★★

ernest jackson
our love will always be the same

value — $
rarity — ◆◆◆◆◆
quality — ★★★

george smith
don't find me guilty

value — $
rarity — ◆◆◆
quality — ★★★

flash mc kinley
i'll rescue you

value — $$$
rarity — ◆◆◆◆
quality — ★★★★★

fascinators
in other words

value — $$$
rarity — ◆◆◆◆
quality — ★★★★★

magnetics
lady in green

value	rarity	quality
$$$$	◆◆◆◆	★★★★★

mary johnson
i'm tired

value	rarity	quality
$	◆◆◆◆	★★★

natural four
hanging on to a lie

value	rarity	quality
$	◆	★★★★

natural four
i thought you were mine

value	rarity	quality
$	◆◆	★★★★

carol mogan
i've got everything

value	rarity	quality
$$	♦♦♦♦	★★★

reggie alexander
it's better

value	rarity	quality
$	♦♦♦	★★★★

celebrities
i choose you baby

value	rarity	quality
$$$	♦♦♦♦	★★★★

changing times
a new day begins

value	rarity	quality
$$$	♦♦♦♦♦	★★★★

inspirations
no one else can take your place

value	rarity	quality
$$$$$	♦♦♦♦♦	★★★★★

harriet laverne & the lovenote
a letter to my love

value	rarity	quality
$$	♦♦♦♦	★★★

ebo-nees
doll age

value	rarity	quality
$$$	♦♦♦♦♦	★★★

ellipsis
people

value	rarity	quality
$$	♦♦♦♦	★★★★

mark IV
if you can't tell me something good

value	rarity	quality
$$	♦♦♦	★★★★★

ben iverson & the nue dey express
i tried my best

value	rarity	quality
$	♦♦♦♦	★★★

curtis anderson
the hardest part

value	rarity	quality
$	♦♦	★★★★★

ultimates
girl i've been trying to tell you

value	rarity	quality
$	♦	★★★★

buddy smith
when you lose the one you love

value	rarity	quality
$$$	♦♦♦♦	★★★★★

tokays
baby, baby, baby

value	rarity	quality
$$	♦♦♦	★★★★

empires
you're on top girl

value	rarity	quality
$$$	♦♦♦♦	★★★★★

carletts
i'm getting tired

value	rarity	quality
$	♦♦	★★★★

corey blake
how can i go on without you

value	rarity	quality
$	♦♦	★★★★

videls
ain't gonna do you no good

value	rarity	quality
$$	♦♦♦	★★★

ty karim
lighten up baby

value	rarity	quality
$	♦♦♦	★★★★★

jillettes
please say you'll love me

value	rarity	quality
$$	♦♦♦♦	★★★★

gambrells
pain in my heart

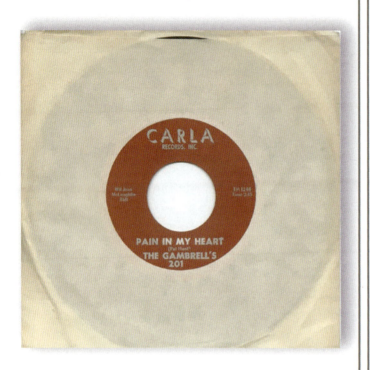

value	rarity	quality
$	♦♦♦	★★★

jimmy delphs
dancing a hole in the world

value	rarity	quality
$$$	♦♦♦♦♦	★★★★

sy hightower
i know you're leaving me

value	rarity	quality
$$	♦♦♦	★★★★★

purple mundi
stop hurting me baby

value	rarity	quality
$$	♦♦♦	★★★★★

blue steam
i want a girl

value   rarity   quality
$ ♦♦♦   ★★★

fred & the turbins
bernadine

value   rarity   quality
$$$ ♦♦♦♦   ★★★★

turbines
what more can i stay

value   rarity   quality
$ ♦♦♦   ★★

topics
hey girl (where are you going)

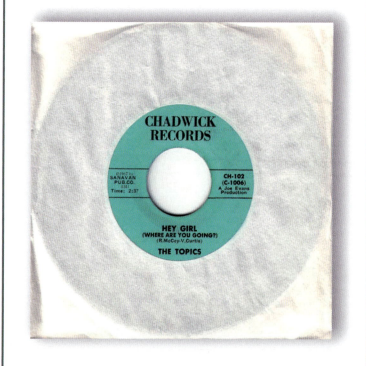

value   rarity   quality
$ ♦♦♦   ★★★★

paul vann
one track mind

value	rarity	quality
$	♦♦♦	★★★

burning desire
why she had to go

value	rarity	quality
$	♦♦♦	★★★

servicemen
connie

value	rarity	quality
$$	♦♦♦	★★★★★

sterophonics
run on little girl

value	rarity	quality
$	♦♦♦	★★★

hyperions
why you wanna treat me the way you do

value   rarity   quality
$$ ♦♦♦   ★★★★

chantlers
in the beginning

value   rarity   quality
$$ ♦♦♦♦   ★★★★

tony clarke
landslide

value   rarity   quality
$$ ♦♦♦♦   ★★★★★

willie dee
it looks like rain

value   rarity   quality
$ ♦♦♦♦   ★★

cole & the grandures
i need you

value	rarity	quality
$$$$	♦♦♦♦♦	★★★★

vise
baby, i love you

value	rarity	quality
$$	♦♦♦	★★★★

johnny james
tell you about my girl

value	rarity	quality
$$	♦♦♦	★★★★

romona collins
you've been cheating

value	rarity	quality
$$$	♦♦♦	★★★★

buster and eddie
can't be still

value   rarity   quality
$ ♦♦♦   ★★★★★

milton parker
women like it harder

value   rarity   quality
$$ ♦♦♦   ★★★★★

george pepp
the feeling is real

value   rarity   quality
$$$$ ♦♦♦♦♦   ★★★★★

unique
don't you be no fool

value   rarity   quality
$ ♦♦♦♦   ★★★★

greater experience
don't forget to remember

value	rarity	quality
$	♦♦	★★★★

cookie woodson
i'll be true

value	rarity	quality
$$	♦♦♦	★★★★

chandlers
your love makes me lonely

value	rarity	quality
$	♦	★★★★

liz verdi
you let him get away

value	rarity	quality
$	♦♦♦	★★★★

jimmy fraser
of hopes and dreams and tombstones

value	rarity	quality
$	◆	★★★

voices, incorporated
thinkin'

value	rarity	quality
$	◆	★★★

dana valery
you don't know where your interest lies

value	rarity	quality
$	◆	★★★

billy thompson
black-eyed girl

value	rarity	quality
$	◆◆	★★★

patterson twins
gonna find a true love

value $ rarity ♦♦   quality ★★★★

adventurers
easy baby

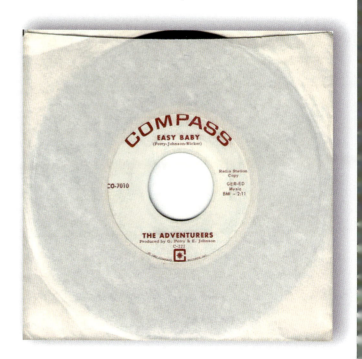

value $ rarity ♦   quality ★★★★

7th avenue aviators
you should 'o held on

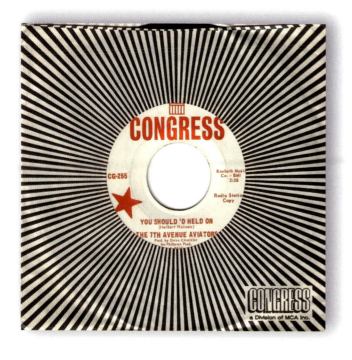

value $$ rarity ♦♦   quality ★★★★

anita anderson
secretly

value $ rarity ♦♦♦♦   quality ★★★

paulette
love you babe

value	rarity	quality
$$$	♦♦♦♦	★★★★

danny woods
you had me fooled

value	rarity	quality
$	♦♦	★★★★

delores johnson, les watson and the panthers
it hurts me so bad

value	rarity	quality
$	♦♦♦♦	★★

betty turner
the winds kept laughing

value	rarity	quality
$	♦♦♦	★★★★

joseph webster
my love is so strong

value rarity quality
$$$ ♦♦♦♦♦   ★★★★★

exquisites
just couldn't make it

value rarity quality
$$$ ♦♦♦♦♦   ★★★★

de-lites
lover

value rarity quality
$$$ ♦♦♦   ★★★★★

thornton sisters
i keep forgettin'

value rarity quality
$$$ ♦♦♦♦   ★★★★

profs
look at you

value	rarity	quality
$$	◆◆◆◆	★★★

robert sanders
what i don't see can't hurt me

value	rarity	quality
$	◆◆◆	★★★

johnnie elby
it's alright but it's wrong

value	rarity	quality
$$	◆◆◆◆◆	★★★★

earl white jr.
very special girl

value	rarity	quality
$$	◆◆◆◆	★★★★

jimmie 'bo' horn
i can't speak

value	rarity	quality
$$$	◆◆◆◆	★★★★★

twans
i can't see him again

value	rarity	quality
$$$	◆◆◆◆	★★★★

frankie and the damons
bad woman

value	rarity	quality
$	◆◆◆◆	★★★

camaro's
we're not too young

value	rarity	quality
$$$	◆◆◆◆	★★★★

timeless legend
i was born to love you (part one)

value $$
rarity ◆◆◆
quality ★★★★★

betty wilson & the 4 bars
i'm yours

value $$$
rarity ◆◆◆◆
quality ★★★★

7 nombres
listen people

value $
rarity ◆◆◆◆
quality ★★★

d.c. magnatones
does she love me

value $$$$
rarity ◆◆◆◆◆
quality ★★★★

moments
you said

value	rarity	quality
$$$	♦♦♦♦	★★★★

gloria hill
be somebody

value	rarity	quality
$$	♦♦♦♦	★★

betty wright
paralyzed

value	rarity	quality
$	♦♦♦♦	★★

jesse butler
it's my business

value	rarity	quality
$	♦♦♦♦♦	★★★★

vashons
we'll be together

value	rarity	quality
$$	♦♦♦♦♦	★★★

masters
(i'm) just a man in love

value	rarity	quality
$	♦♦	★★★★

oxford nights
i'm such a lonely one

value	rarity	quality
$	♦♦	★★★

parisians
twinkle little star

value	rarity	quality
$	♦♦♦	★★★★

ivorys
please stay

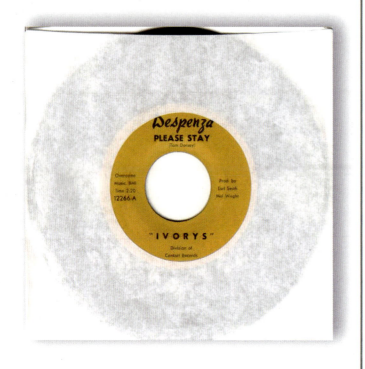

value	rarity	quality
$$	♦♦♦	★★★★★

valiants
tell me, tell me what you gonna do

value	rarity	quality
$	♦♦♦♦	★★★

ronnie mc neir
sitting in my class

value	rarity	quality
$$	♦♦♦	★★★★★

sequins
try my love

value	rarity	quality
$$	♦♦♦♦	★★★★

tempos
i'll never forget

value **$$** rarity ♦♦♦♦ quality ★★★★★

stepstones
lonely one

value **$** rarity ♦♦♦ quality ★★★★

international iv
equal love

value **$$** rarity ♦♦♦♦♦ quality ★★★

liz verdi
ten good reasons why i won't sleep tonight

value **$** rarity ♦♦♦♦♦ quality ★★★★

little stanley lippett
out of sight lovin'

value	rarity	quality
$$$	◆◆◆◆◆	★★★★

clyde milton
i'd rather leave on my feet

value	rarity	quality
$$	◆◆◆◆	★★★★

vicki nelson
stoney face

value	rarity	quality
$	◆◆◆	★★★

visitors
little golden band

value	rarity	quality
$$	◆◆◆◆◆	★★

paris
sleepless nights

value: $$$
rarity: ♦♦♦
quality: ★★★★★

sandy wynns
touch of venus

value: $
rarity: ♦♦♦
quality: ★★★★★

royal playboys
arabia

value: $
rarity: ♦♦♦
quality: ★★★

dave charles
ain't gonna cry no more

value: $$
rarity: ♦♦♦
quality: ★★★★

blendels
you need love

value	rarity	quality
$$$	♦♦♦♦	★★★★★

contemplations
alone with no love

value	rarity	quality
$$	♦♦♦	★★★★

milton james
my lonely feeling

value	rarity	quality
$$$	♦♦♦♦♦	★★★

eddie kool
i look in the mirror

value	rarity	quality
$	♦♦♦	★★

rita & the tiaras
gone with the wind is my love

value	rarity	quality
$$	♦♦♦	★★★★★

reatha reese
only lies

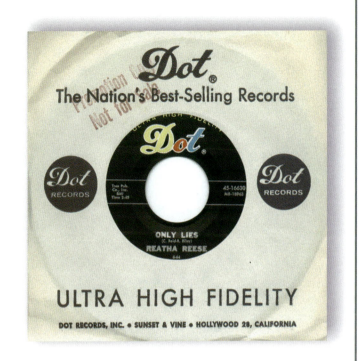

value	rarity	quality
$	♦♦♦	★★★

johnny hampton
not my girl

value	rarity	quality
$$	♦♦♦	★★★★★

gail nevels
taking my mind off love

value	rarity	quality
$$$	♦♦♦♦	★★★★

little rodger hatcher
i need you

value	rarity	quality
$	♦♦♦♦	★★★

carl (soul dog) marshall
i can't live without you

value	rarity	quality
$$	♦♦♦♦♦	★★★★★

dolly gilmore
sweet sweet baby

value	rarity	quality
$$	♦♦♦	★★★

don varner
here come my tears

value	rarity	quality
$$	♦♦♦♦♦	★★★

topics
have your fun

value — $$$ rarity — ◆◆◆◆   quality — ★★★★

dreamettes
that's not love

value — $$ rarity — ◆◆◆◆◆   quality — ★★★

precisions
sugar ain't sweet

value — $$$$ rarity — ◆◆◆◆◆   quality — ★★★★

precisions
i wanna tell my baby

value — $$$ rarity — ◆◆◆◆   quality — ★★★★

cody black
mr blue

value rarity quality
$ ♦♦   ★★★

willie hutch
love runs out

value rarity quality
$$ ♦♦♦♦   ★★★★★

brand new
thousand years

value rarity quality
$$ ♦♦♦   ★★★

c coulter
i can't fight the feeling

value rarity quality
$$$ ♦♦♦♦   ★★★★

stanley mitchell
get it baby

value — $
rarity — ♦♦♦
quality — ★★★★

larry clinton
she's wanted

value — $$$
rarity — ♦♦♦♦
quality — ★★★★★

coco and ben
good feelin

value — $$
rarity — ♦♦♦♦
quality — ★★★★

unique blend
yes i'm in love

value — $
rarity — ♦♦
quality — ★★★★

court davis
try to think (what you're doing)

value	rarity	quality
$$$	♦♦♦	★★★★

willie pickett
on the stage of life

value	rarity	quality
$$	♦♦♦♦	★★★★

barry scruggs
after all (you put me thru)

value	rarity	quality
$	♦♦♦	★★★

tommy turner
lazy

value	rarity	quality
$	♦♦♦	★★★★

troy dodds
try my love

value $$
rarity ♦♦
quality ★★★★

passions
if you see my baby

value $$$
rarity ♦♦♦♦
quality ★★★★

maureen bailey
takin' my time with you

value $$
rarity ♦♦♦♦
quality ★★★

anthony & the delsonics
every time

value $$
rarity ♦♦♦
quality ★★★

elsie strong
you cut the love line

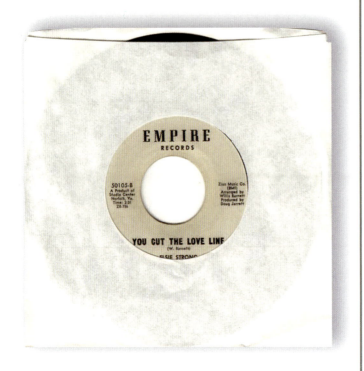

value: $$
rarity: ♦♦♦♦
quality: ★★★

endeavors
i can't help crying

value: $
rarity: ♦♦♦
quality: ★★★

lenny curtis
nothing can help you now

value: $$
rarity: ♦♦
quality: ★★★★★

doll face
please return

value: $$
rarity: ♦♦♦♦♦
quality: ★★★

jewel akens
my first lonely night

value rarity quality
$ ♦♦ ★★★

steve flanagan
i've arrived

value rarity quality
$$ ♦♦ ★★★

jesse davis
gonna hang on in there girl

value rarity quality
$$$ ♦♦♦ ★★★★

jimmy burns
i really love you

value rarity quality
$$$$ ♦♦♦♦ ★★★★★

patti young
head and shoulders (above the rest)

value	rarity	quality
$$	♦♦♦	★★★★

rufus wood
before 2001

value	rarity	quality
$$	♦♦♦	★★★★

big don's rebellion
it was true

value	rarity	quality
$	♦♦	★★★★★

blueprints
i want something when i need money

value	rarity	quality
$$	♦♦♦♦	★★★

hank hodge
eye for an eye

value	rarity	quality
$$$	♦♦♦♦♦	★★★★

hank hodge
one way love

value	rarity	quality
$$	♦♦♦	★★★

charles sheffield
it's your voodoo working

value	rarity	quality
$	♦	★★★★

frankie beverly & the butlers
because of my heart

value	rarity	quality
$$$	♦♦♦♦	★★★★★

damon fox
packing up

value	rarity	quality
$$$$	◆◆◆◆◆	★★★★★

pat & the blenders
(all i need is your) good, good lovin

value	rarity	quality
$	◆◆◆	★★★

andy fisher
my heart's beating stronger

value	rarity	quality
$$$	◆◆◆◆	★★★★★

leon haywood
baby reconsider

value	rarity	quality
$$	◆◆	★★★★★

claudine clark
goodbye mama

value	rarity	quality
$	♦♦♦♦	★★★

thomas bailey
wish i was back

value	rarity	quality
$$$	♦♦♦♦	★★★★★

soul communicaters
those lonely nights

value	rarity	quality
$$	♦	★★★★★

foxes
mighty good sign

value	rarity	quality
$	♦♦♦♦	★★

jimmy ricks
oh! what a feeling

value rarity quality
$ ♦♦ ★★★★

flirtations
stronger than her love

value rarity quality
$ ♦♦ ★★★★★

cal green
i'll give you just a little more time

value rarity quality
$ ♦♦♦ ★★★

five chances
stranger i love you

value rarity quality
$$ ♦♦♦♦ ★★★

rayons
you confuse me baby

value	rarity	quality
$	♦♦♦	★★★

mel britt
she'll come running back

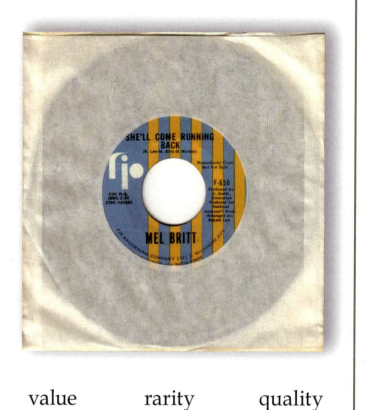

value	rarity	quality
$$	♦♦♦	★★★★★

clay brown
nothing but love

value	rarity	quality
$$	♦♦♦♦♦	★★★★

tranells
blessed with a love

value	rarity	quality
$$$	♦♦♦♦	★★★★

antellects
love slave

value	rarity	quality
$$$	♦♦♦♦♦	★★★★

inconquerables
for your love

value	rarity	quality
$$$	♦♦♦♦♦	★★★

kenny smith & the loveliters
one more day

value	rarity	quality
$	♦♦♦	★★★

kenny smith & the loveliters
go for your self

value	rarity	quality
$	♦♦♦	★★★

len jewell
bettin' on love

value	rarity	quality
$	♦♦♦	★★★★★

rotations
put a dime on d-9

value	rarity	quality
$	♦♦♦	★★★

rotations
a changed man

value	rarity	quality
$	♦♦♦	★★★★

lovers
without a doubt

value	rarity	quality
$$$	♦♦♦♦	★★★★

imaginations
strange neighbourhood

value: $
rarity: ♦♦
quality: ★★★

leroy barbour
i ain't going nowhere

value: $$
rarity: ♦♦♦♦
quality: ★★★★

chico lamarr
what do you think i am

value: $$$
rarity: ♦♦♦♦
quality: ★★★★

al mason
good lovin

value: $$
rarity: ♦♦♦
quality: ★★★

ronnie walker
now there is you

value: $
rarity: ♦♦♦
quality: ★★

mikie and the ardons
three's a crowd

value: $
rarity: ♦♦♦
quality: ★★

frank beverly
if that's what you wanted

value: $
rarity: ♦♦
quality: ★★★★★

garland green
girl i love you

value: $$
rarity: ♦♦♦♦
quality: ★★★★★

just brothers
carlena

value	rarity	quality
$$$	♦♦♦	★★★★

honey bees
let's get back together

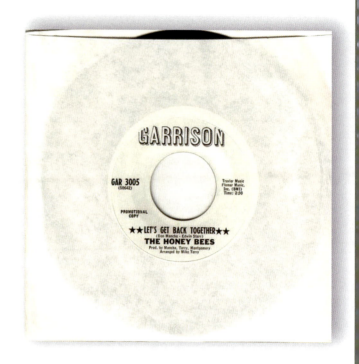

value	rarity	quality
$$$	♦♦♦	★★★★

willie tee
i'm having so much fun

value	rarity	quality
$$	♦♦♦♦	★★★★

willie tee
first taste of hurt

value	rarity	quality
$	♦♦♦	★★★★★

lynn varnado
wash and wear love

value	rarity	quality
$$$	♦♦♦♦	★★★★★

big bo and the four m's
i've got to go

value	rarity	quality
$$	♦♦♦♦	★★★

ella thomas & dollets
thing called love

value	rarity	quality
$	♦♦♦	★★

fuller bros
stranger at my door

value	rarity	quality
$	♦♦♦	★★

benny harper
don't let it happen to you

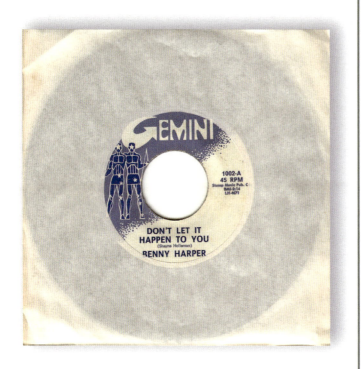

value	rarity	quality
$	◆◆◆◆◆	★★★

wombat
i'm gettin' on life

value	rarity	quality
$	◆◆◆◆	★★★

jimmie braswell
i can't give you my heart

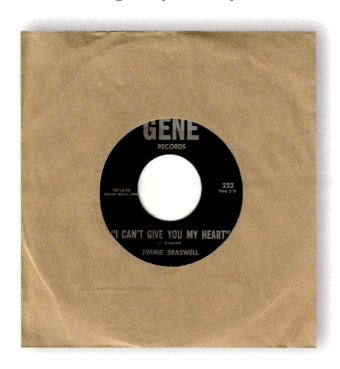

value	rarity	quality
$$	◆◆◆◆	★★★★

charles burns
i love my baby

value	rarity	quality
$	◆◆◆◆	★★★

margaret little
i need some loving

value   rarity   quality
$$$$ ◆◆◆◆◆   ★★★★

al scott
what happened to yesterday

value   rarity   quality
$$$ ◆◆◆◆◆   ★★★★★

mr. soul
what happened to yesterday

value   rarity   quality
$$$ ◆◆◆◆◆   ★★★★★

cody black
it's our time to fall in love

value   rarity   quality
$$$ ◆◆◆◆◆   ★★

carbon copies
just don't love you

value	rarity	quality
$$	♦♦♦♦	★★★★

rodger wade
tell me what they say

value	rarity	quality
$$$	♦♦♦♦♦	★★★

jerry washington
don't waste my time

value	rarity	quality
$	♦♦♦	★★★★

chuck holiday
just can't trust nobody

value	rarity	quality
$$$	♦♦♦♦	★★★★★

georgetta banks
sweetly and completely

value — $
rarity — ♦♦
quality — ★★

little john
just wait and see

value — $$$
rarity — ♦♦♦♦♦
quality — ★★★★★

shametts
don't waste your time

value — $
rarity — ♦♦
quality — ★★★

soul bros inc.
pyramid

value — $$
rarity — ♦
quality — ★★★★★

ozz and his sperlings
can you qualify

value	rarity	quality
$	♦♦	★★★

chuck wells
the love knot

value	rarity	quality
$	♦♦♦	★★★

kenny smith
lord what's happened

value	rarity	quality
$	♦♦♦	★★★

ruby
feminine ingenuity

value	rarity	quality
$	♦♦♦	★★★★

nat t. jones
moving forward

value: $$
rarity: ◆◆◆◆
quality: ★★★

spider turner
i've got to get myself together (before i lose my mind)

value: $
rarity: ◆
quality: ★★★★

silhouettes
not me baby

value: $$
rarity: ◆◆
quality: ★★★★★

teardrops
wait for me

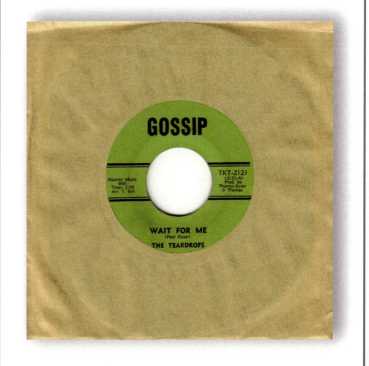

value: $$$
rarity: ◆◆◆◆◆
quality: ★★★★

blue sharks
these things will keep me loving you

value $$
rarity ◆◆◆◆
quality ★★★

larry allen
can't we talk it over

value $$
rarity ◆◆◆◆
quality ★★★★

tony borders
cheaters never win

value $$
rarity ◆◆◆◆◆
quality ★★★★

bernard smith & jokers wild
gotta be a reason

value $$
rarity ◆◆◆
quality ★★★★

professionals
that's why i love you

value: $$$$ rarity: ♦♦♦♦♦ quality: ★★★★★

fred briggs
sound off

value: $ rarity: ♦♦♦ quality: ★★★★

sam ward
sister lee

value: $$ rarity: ♦♦♦ quality: ★★★★★

steve mancha
friday night

value: $ rarity: ♦ quality: ★★★★★

exceptions
the look in her eyes

value $$
rarity ♦♦♦
quality ★★★★★

anderson brothers
i can see him loving you

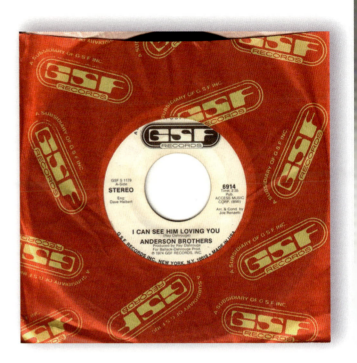

value $$
rarity ♦♦♦♦♦
quality ★★★★★

connie laverne
can't live without you

value $
rarity ♦♦♦♦
quality ★★★★

primers
how does it grab you

value $$$
rarity ♦♦♦♦♦
quality ★★★★

benny harper
my prayer

value	rarity	quality
$$	♦♦♦	★★★

david gage
can i depend on you

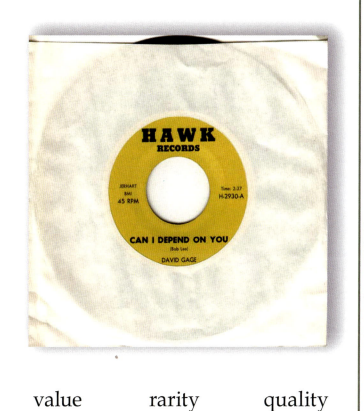

value	rarity	quality
$$	♦♦♦♦♦	★★★

detroit sounds of friction
i'm leaving you

value	rarity	quality
$$$	♦♦♦♦	★★★★

eddie billups
shake off that dream

value	rarity	quality
$	♦♦♦♦	★★★★

cashmeres
show stopper

value	rarity	quality
$$$	♦♦♦	★★★★★

glenda mc leod
no stranger to love

value	rarity	quality
$$	♦♦♦♦♦	★★★★

luther ingram
if it's all the same to you babe

value	rarity	quality
$$	♦♦♦♦	★★★★★

kell osborne
a law against a heartbreaker

value	rarity	quality
$$$$	♦♦♦♦♦	★★★

overtones
what would i do

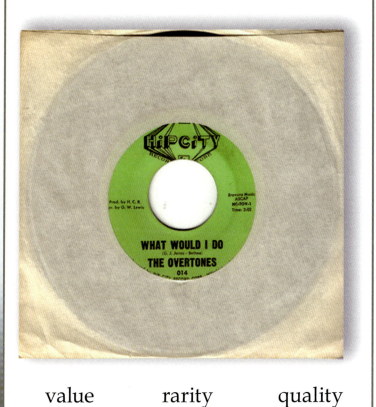

value $$$ rarity ◆◆◆◆◆ quality ★★★

royal cinders
girl you sure is funky

value $$$ rarity ◆◆◆◆◆ quality ★★★

psychodelic frankie
putting you out of my life

value $$ rarity ◆◆◆ quality ★★★

zeke and the soul setters
make my love a hurtin thing

value $ rarity ◆◆◆ quality ★★★

quiet fire
lost (without your love)

value $
rarity ◆◆◆◆◆
quality ★★

gary griffin & the top ten
think nothing about it

value $
rarity ◆◆◆◆◆
quality ★★

moments
baby i want you

value $$$$
rarity ◆◆◆◆◆
quality ★★★★★

hollidays
set me on my feet right

value $$
rarity ◆◆◆◆
quality ★★★

billy arnell
tough girl

value	rarity	quality
$$$	♦♦♦	★★★

sherrys
put your arms around me

value	rarity	quality
$$	♦♦♦	★★★★

little joe cook
i'm falling in love with you baby

value	rarity	quality
$$	♦♦♦	★★★★

sonatas
going on down the road

value	rarity	quality
$$$	♦♦♦♦	★★★

60's Record Company 45 Mailers

60's Record Company 45 Mailers

gerri hall
who can i run to

value   rarity   quality
$$ ◆   ★★★

donna king
take me home

value   rarity   quality
$$ ◆◆   ★★★★

tommy jones & swinging pharoahs
come home to me

value   rarity   quality
$$ ◆◆◆◆◆   ★★★★

wilson williams
i got a whole lot to be thankful for

value   rarity   quality
$ ◆◆◆◆   ★★

duke browner
crying over you

value: $
rarity: ◆
quality: ★★★★★

jock mitchell
not a chance in a million

value: $
rarity: ◆
quality: ★★★★

nabay
believe it or not

value: $$$
rarity: ◆◆◆◆
quality: ★★★★

ann sexton & the masters of soul
you've been gone too long

value: $$
rarity: ◆◆◆◆
quality: ★★★★★

fantastics
where there's a will there's a way

value	rarity	quality
$$	♦	★★★★

eddie foster
i never knew

value	rarity	quality
$	♦	★★★★★

calvin grayson
love just begun

value	rarity	quality
$$	♦♦♦	★★★★

dena barnes
if you ever walk out of my life

value	rarity	quality
$$	♦	★★★★★

crow
your autumn of tomorrow

value	rarity	quality
$$	♦♦♦	★★★★★

dennis edwards
johnnie on the spot

value	rarity	quality
$$$$	♦♦♦♦♦	★★★★★

tommy ridgley
my love gets stronger

value	rarity	quality
$$$	♦♦♦♦	★★★★★

sheppard boy
my angel baby

value	rarity	quality
$	♦	★★

poets
wrapped around your finger

value	rarity	quality
$$$	♦♦♦♦	★★★★★

stewart ames
angelina, oh angelina

value	rarity	quality
$$	♦♦	★★★

jackey beaver
lover come back

value	rarity	quality
$$	♦♦♦♦	★★★

debbie curtis
i check my mail box

value	rarity	quality
$$	♦♦♦♦	★★

paul smith
i'll run

value	rarity	quality
$	♦♦	★★★

melvin davis
about love

value	rarity	quality
$$	♦♦♦♦♦	★★

johnny moore
just be for real

value	rarity	quality
$	♦♦♦	★★★

spencer sterling
come back to me

value	rarity	quality
$$$	♦♦♦♦♦	★★★★

dem III
i got a woman

value rarity quality
$ ♦♦♦♦♦ ★★

bell boys
i don't want to lose you

value rarity quality
$ ♦♦♦ ★★★

matt brown
everyday (i love you just a little bit more)

value rarity quality
$$ ♦♦♦♦ ★★★

matt brown
thank you baby

value rarity quality
$$ ♦♦♦♦ ★★★

sandra stephens
if you really love me

value: $
rarity: ♦♦♦
quality: ★★★

blue jays
point of view

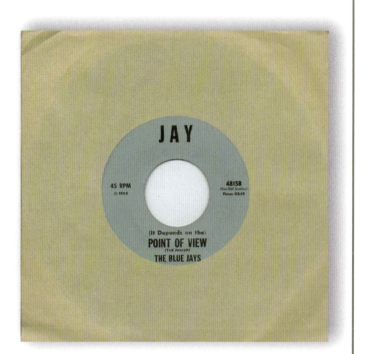

value: $$
rarity: ♦♦♦
quality: ★★★★

richard caiton
where is the love

value: $$
rarity: ♦♦♦
quality: ★★★

cynthia sheeler
i'll cry over you (pt.1)

value: $$
rarity: ♦♦♦♦
quality: ★★★

colt 45's
lady lady

value	rarity	quality
$$	♦♦♦	★★

jesse davis
so full of love

value	rarity	quality
$$	♦♦♦♦	★★

barbara long
take it from me

value	rarity	quality
$$	♦♦♦♦	★★★

jimmy castor
it's ok

value	rarity	quality
$	♦♦♦	★★

chryslers with the monarchs band
i'm not gonna lose you

value	rarity	quality
$$	♦♦♦	★★★

b.j. thomas
keep it up

value	rarity	quality
$	♦♦	★★

connie clark
my sugar baby

value	rarity	quality
$	♦♦	★★★★★

showmen
need love

value	rarity	quality
$	♦♦♦	★★

les mack and the impacts
so blue

value	rarity	quality
$$	♦♦♦	★★

eptones
a love that's real

value	rarity	quality
$	♦♦♦	★★

norma and the heartaches
nice and slow

value	rarity	quality
$$	♦♦♦♦	★★★

sound-masters
lonely lonely

value	rarity	quality
$$	♦♦♦	★★★★

arthur freeman
you got me up tight

value	rarity	quality
$$	♦♦♦	★★★

bobby 'guitar' bennett
you did it again

value	rarity	quality
$	♦♦♦	★★★

lyrics
thoughts of a summer day

value	rarity	quality
$	♦♦♦	★★

willy mason
why

value	rarity	quality
$$	♦♦♦	★★★

target
give me one more chance

value	rarity	quality
$$	♦♦♦♦	★★★

isonics
sugar

value	rarity	quality
$$	♦♦	★★★

paul & paula
i've got something on my mind

value	rarity	quality
$$	♦♦♦♦	★★★

helen troy
i think i love you

value	rarity	quality
$	♦	★★★

rubin
you've been away

value: $
rarity: ♦♦♦
quality: ★★★★★

patti & the emblems
i'm gonna love you a long, long time

value: $
rarity: ♦
quality: ★★★★★

exits
another sundown in watts

value: $
rarity: ♦
quality: ★★★★

september jones
i'm coming home

value: $$
rarity: ♦♦♦
quality: ★★★★★

volumes
ain't gonna give you up

value	rarity	quality
$$	♦♦♦	★★★

sharon mc mahan
here comes that boy i love

value	rarity	quality
$$	♦♦♦♦	★★★

sharon mc mann
got to find another guy

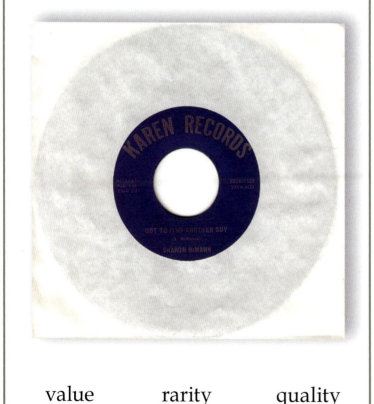

value	rarity	quality
$	♦♦♦	★★

matt lucas
baby you better go-go

value	rarity	quality
$$$	♦♦♦♦	★★★

mikki farrow
set my heart at ease

value	rarity	quality
$$	♦♦♦	★★★★★

stemmons express
woman, love thief

value	rarity	quality
$$	♦♦♦	★★★

bobby james
i really love you

value	rarity	quality
$$$$	♦♦♦♦♦	★★★★

seville
show me the way

value	rarity	quality
$$	♦♦♦♦	★★★★

soul sisters
you can't be my boy-friend

value	rarity	quality
$$	♦♦♦♦	★★★

cliffhangers
since you've gone away

value	rarity	quality
$$	♦♦♦♦♦	★★★

eugene smiley
yes it's you

value	rarity	quality
$$	♦♦♦♦	★★★★★

timmy carr
workin'

value	rarity	quality
$$$	♦♦♦♦♦	★★★★

la wanda william
come back to me

value: $$$
rarity: ◆◆◆◆◆
quality: ★★★

melvin davis
it's no news

value: $$$
rarity: ◆◆◆◆◆
quality: ★★★

c.o.d.'s
she's fire

value: $$$$
rarity: ◆◆◆◆◆
quality: ★★★

combinations
what' cha gonna do

value: $$$$
rarity: ◆◆◆◆◆
quality: ★★★★★

c.o.d.'s
coming back girl

value	rarity	quality
$$	♦♦	★★★

little jimmy edwards
slapping some soul upon me

value	rarity	quality
$$	♦♦♦	★★★★★

electric express
hear say i

value	rarity	quality
$$	♦♦♦♦	★★★

mary wright
i was a fool

value	rarity	quality
$	♦♦♦♦	★★

junior mc cants
try me for your love

value: $$$$
rarity: ♦♦♦♦♦
quality: ★★★★★

t.c. lee & the bricklayers
up and down the hill

value: $$
rarity: ♦♦♦
quality: ★★★

cody black
i'm slowly molding

value: $$
rarity: ♦♦♦
quality: ★★★★★

roosevelt matthews with billy ball & upsetters
you got me diggin' you

value: $$
rarity: ♦♦♦
quality: ★★★★★

combinations
i'm gonna make you love me

value	rarity	quality
$$$	♦♦♦♦	★★★★★

jimmie raye
philly dog around the world

value	rarity	quality
$	♦♦♦	★★★★

other ones
the two of us

value	rarity	quality
$	♦♦	★★

ernie rivers
a message to percy

value	rarity	quality
$$	♦♦♦♦♦	★★★★★

tommy tate
if you got to love somebody

value   rarity   quality
$$ ♦♦♦♦♦   ★★★★

little dooley
if ever i needed you

value   rarity   quality
$ ♦   ★★★

joe matthews
ain't nothing you can do

value   rarity   quality
$$$ ♦♦♦   ★★★★★

inmates
this is the day

value   rarity   quality
$$ ♦♦♦♦   ★★★

frank foster & the l.a. untouchables
my assurance

value: $
rarity: ♦♦♦
quality: ★★★

robby lawson
burning sensation

value: $$$
rarity: ♦♦♦♦
quality: ★★★★

al williams
i am nothing

value: $$$
rarity: ♦♦♦♦
quality: ★★★★★

masqueraders
how

value: $$
rarity: ♦♦
quality: ★★★★★

lester tipton
this won't change

value   rarity   quality
$$$$ ♦♦♦♦   ★★★★★

ernest mosley
stubborn heart

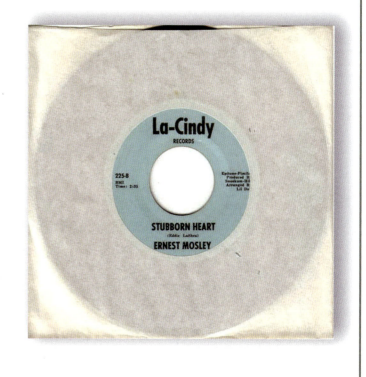

value   rarity   quality
$$ ♦♦♦   ★★★★★

walter & the admerations
man oh man (what have i done)

value   rarity   quality
$$$$ ♦♦♦♦♦   ★★★

ellusions
you didn't have to leave

value   rarity   quality
$ ♦   ★★★★★

vaguards
good times bad times

value	rarity	quality
$$$	♦♦♦	★★★★★

pearls
shooting high

value	rarity	quality
$	♦♦♦	★★★

antiques
go for yourself

value	rarity	quality
$$$	♦♦♦	★★★

lynn terry
i got a good thing goin'

value	rarity	quality
$$$	♦♦♦♦♦	★★

utopias
girls are against me

value — rarity — quality
$$$ — ◆◆◆◆ — ★★★

gwen owens
make him mine

value — rarity — quality
$ — ◆◆◆ — ★★★

george smith
pretty little girl

value — rarity — quality
$ — ◆◆◆◆ — ★★★

modern redcaps
empty world

value — rarity — quality
$ — ◆◆◆ — ★★★

john leach
put that woman down

value	rarity	quality
$$	♦♦♦	★★★★

oliver christian
dissatisfied man

value	rarity	quality
$$	♦♦♦♦	★★★

jerry and his uniques
yes he will

value	rarity	quality
$	♦♦♦	★★

lil lavair and the fabulous jades
i'll be so happy

value	rarity	quality
$$	♦♦♦♦	★★★

blenders
cause i love you

value	rarity	quality
$$	♦♦♦	★★★

betty o'brian
she'll be gone

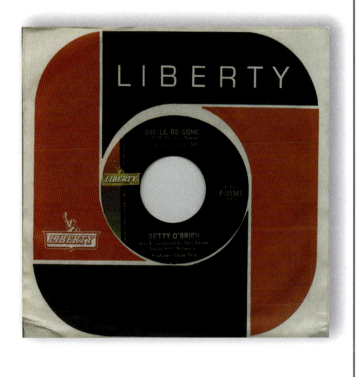

value	rarity	quality
$	♦	★★★

agents
trouble

value	rarity	quality
$	♦♦♦	★★★★

nathan williams
what price

value	rarity	quality
$$	♦♦♦	★★★★

jeanie & the gentlemen
let me down easy

value	rarity	quality
$$	♦♦♦♦	★★★

majestics
(i love her so much) it hurts me

value	rarity	quality
$$	♦	★★★★★

illusions
walking boy

value	rarity	quality
$	♦♦♦	★★

paul kelly
the upset

value	rarity	quality
$$$	♦♦♦♦♦	★★★★

freddie chavez
they'll never know why

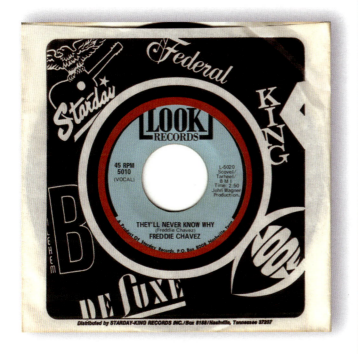

value: $$
rarity: ♦♦♦♦
quality: ★★★★★

hamilton movement
she's gone

value: $$$
rarity: ♦♦♦
quality: ★★★★★

nat hall
why (i want to know)

value: $$
rarity: ♦♦♦
quality: ★★★★

primes
gotta go now

value: $$
rarity: ♦♦♦♦
quality: ★★

bishop
you can't take it with you

value: $$
rarity: ◆◆◆◆
quality: ★★★★★

headlines
he's looking for a love

value: $$
rarity: ◆◆◆
quality: ★★★

brand new faces
brand new faces

value: $$$
rarity: ◆◆◆◆
quality: ★★★

rhythm machine
put a smile on time

value: $$
rarity: ◆◆◆◆
quality: ★★★★★

executive four
i gotta good thing going and i ain't gonna blow it

value: $$$ rarity: ♦♦♦♦ quality: ★★★★★

just bros
sliced tomatoes

value: $$ rarity: ♦♦♦♦ quality: ★★★★★

little willie faulk
look into my heart

value: $$$$ rarity: ♦♦♦♦♦ quality: ★★★

mind & matter
i'm under your spell

value: $$ rarity: ♦ quality: ★★★★★

t.j. & the group
blues for the b's

value: $
rarity: ♦♦♦♦
quality: ★★★

clifton walker & the savoys
good thing

value: $
rarity: ♦♦♦
quality: ★★

regents
what 'cha gonna do

value: $
rarity: ♦♦♦♦
quality: ★★★

max uballez
you'd better

value: $
rarity: ♦♦♦♦
quality: ★★

reachers
i just want to do my own thing

value   rarity   quality
$ ♦♦   ★★

s.p.g
loveland

value   rarity   quality
$$ ♦♦   ★★★

mar-j's
got to find a way out

value   rarity   quality
$$ ♦♦♦   ★★★

paramounts
under your spell

value   rarity   quality
$ ♦♦♦   ★★★

ollie jackson
the day my heart stood still

value	rarity	quality
$$	♦♦♦	★★★★★

johnny guitar watson
big bad wolf

value	rarity	quality
$	♦♦♦♦	★★★

tommy dodson III
cooperate

value	rarity	quality
$	♦♦	★★★

clarence hill
a lot of lovin' goin' round

value	rarity	quality
$	♦♦♦	★★★

chuck cockerham
have i got a right

value   rarity   quality
$$ ♦♦♦   ★★★★

don and juan
the heartbreaking truth

value   rarity   quality
$ ♦♦♦   ★★★

timmie williams
competition

value   rarity   quality
$$$ ♦♦♦   ★★★★★

tobi legend
time will pass you by

value   rarity   quality
$$ ♦♦♦   ★★★★★

almeta lattimore
these memories

value $
rarity ♦♦
quality ★★★★

norma jenkins and the dolls
airplane song

value $$$
rarity ♦♦♦♦♦
quality ★★★

magnificents
there can be a better way

value $$
rarity ♦♦♦
quality ★★★★★

four tracks
like my love for you

value $$$
rarity ♦♦♦♦
quality ★★★★★

danny owens
i can't be a fool for you

value	rarity	quality
$$	♦♦♦	★★★

lydia marcelle
it's not like you

value	rarity	quality
$	♦	★★★

moses dillard and the dynamic showmen
pretty as a picture

value	rarity	quality
$$	♦♦	★★★

moses dillard and the dynamic showmen
i'll pay the price

value	rarity	quality
$$	♦♦	★★★★

halo
let me do it

value	rarity	quality
$$	♦♦♦♦	★★★

arthur willis and soulful dynamic's
i've got to find a way

value	rarity	quality
$$$$$	♦♦♦♦♦	★★★★★

roy handy
accidental love

value	rarity	quality
$	♦♦	★★

tamala lewis
you won't say nothing

value	rarity	quality
$$$	♦♦♦	★★★★★

joseph moore
i still can't get you

value	rarity	quality
$$$	♦♦♦	★★★★

blenders
your love has got me down

value	rarity	quality
$$	♦♦♦	★★★

mary lou williams
you know baby

value	rarity	quality
$	♦♦	★★

ralph johnson
have your fun

value	rarity	quality
$	♦♦♦	★★★

ster-phonics
don't leave me

value | rarity | quality
$ | ♦♦♦ | ★★

bobby lee watson
valley of love

value | rarity | quality
$ | ♦♦♦♦ | ★★

bobby kline
say something nice to me

value | rarity | quality
$$ | ♦♦ | ★★★★★

turner bros
let's go fishing

value | rarity | quality
$ | ♦♦♦ | ★★

otis jackson
beggin' for a broken heart

value	rarity	quality
$$	♦♦♦	★★★★

mellow madness
save the youth

value	rarity	quality
$$$	♦♦♦♦	★★★★

robert tanner
sweet memories

value	rarity	quality
$$$	♦♦♦♦	★★★★★

john wesley
love is such a funny thing

value	rarity	quality
$$	♦♦♦♦	★★★★

mello souls
we can make it

value	rarity	quality
$$$$$	♦♦♦♦♦	★★★★★

vandelettes
a love of mine

value	rarity	quality
$	♦♦♦♦	★★

benny scott
no other woman but you

value	rarity	quality
$	♦♦♦♦	★★

royal imperials
this heart of mine

value	rarity	quality
$$$	♦♦♦♦♦	★★★★

toosie rollers
give me love

value	rarity	quality
$	♦♦	★★★

john bowie
you're gonna miss a good thing

value	rarity	quality
$	♦♦	★★★★

vivian carol
oh yeah, yeah, yeah

value	rarity	quality
$$	♦♦	★★

stormie wynters
life saver

value	rarity	quality
$$$	♦♦♦♦	★★★★

jimmy hart
tea house in china town

value **$**   rarity ♦♦   quality ★★★

ella woods
i need your love

value **$$**   rarity ♦♦♦   quality ★★★

edie walker
your unusual love

value **$$**   rarity ♦♦♦   quality ★★★

charades
the key to my happiness

value **$**   rarity ♦   quality ★★★★★

carol and gerri
how can i ever find the way

value   rarity   quality
$ ◆◆◆   ★★★★

dean courtney
you just can't walk away

value   rarity   quality
$ ◆   ★★★★★

andrea henry
i need you like a baby

value   rarity   quality
$ ◆◆◆   ★★★★★

embers
watch out girl

value   rarity   quality
$ ◆◆◆   ★★★★★

catherine young
just because you're a lover (that don't make you a man)

value: $
rarity: ♦♦♦
quality: ★★

gwenn douglass
the picture

value: $
rarity: ♦♦♦
quality: ★★

j.j. barnes
lonely no more

value: $$
rarity: ♦♦♦
quality: ★★★★

inspirations
your wish is my command

value: $$
rarity: ♦♦
quality: ★★★★★

seminoles
you can lump it

value   rarity   quality
$ ♦♦♦   ★★

tearra
just loving you

value   rarity   quality
$$$ ♦♦♦♦   ★★★★★

michael liggins
loaded to the gills pt.1

value   rarity   quality
$ ♦♦♦   ★★★

linda rae
the time to love is now

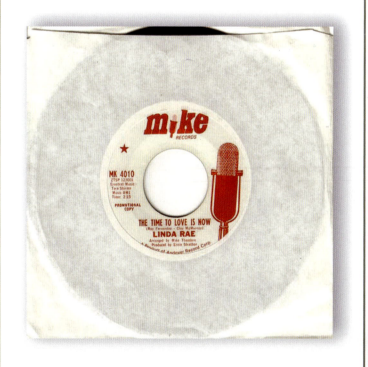

value   rarity   quality
$ ♦♦♦   ★★

karmello brooks
tell me, baby

value	rarity	quality
$$$	♦♦♦	★★★

four reputation
call on me

value	rarity	quality
$	♦♦♦	★★★

buddy ace
color my love

value	rarity	quality
$	♦♦♦♦	★★

shawn robinson
my dear heart

value	rarity	quality
$	♦	★★★★★

ascots
anytime

value rarity quality
$ ♦♦ ★★★

ascots
another day

value rarity quality
$$ ♦♦ ★★★★

joey delorenzo
wake up to the sunshine girl

value rarity quality
$$ ♦♦♦♦ ★★

danny monday
baby, without you

value rarity quality
$$ ♦♦♦ ★★★★★

andantes
hipper, than me

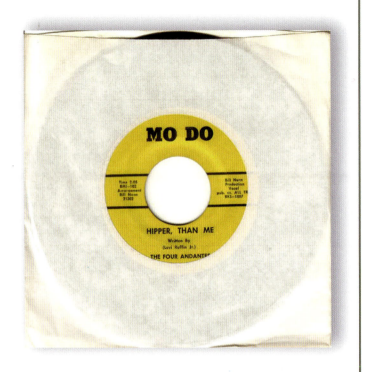

value	rarity	quality
$$$	♦♦♦♦	★★★★

nomads
somethin's bad

value	rarity	quality
$$$	♦♦♦	★★★★

virginia blakly
let nobody love you

value	rarity	quality
$$	♦♦♦	★★★★★

la dellics
i'll never change (my love for you)

value	rarity	quality
$$	♦♦♦♦	★★★

tripplettes
that man of mine

value   rarity   quality
$$ ♦♦♦♦   ★★★

2nd amendment band
backtalk (part one)

value   rarity   quality
$ ♦♦♦   ★★★

mandells
i just can't win

value   rarity   quality
$$ ♦♦♦   ★★★★

charlie mc coy and the escort
my baby's back again

value   rarity   quality
$ ♦♦♦   ★★★

monzas
you know you turn me on

value   rarity   quality
$ ◆   ★★

linda griner
good-by cruel world

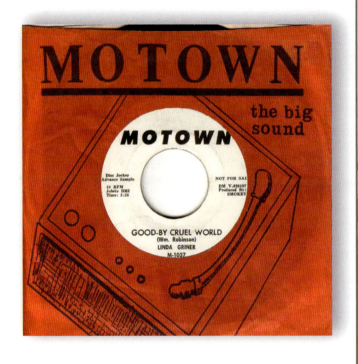

value   rarity   quality
$ ◆◆   ★★★

supremes
a breath taking, first sight soul shaking, one night love making, next day heart breaking guy

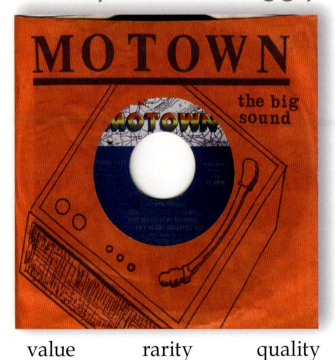

value   rarity   quality
$ ◆◆◆◆   ★★

broomfield corp. jam
doin' it our way

value   rarity   quality
$ ◆◆◆   ★★★

lonnett
blue jeans

value	rarity	quality
$$$	♦♦♦♦	★★★

johnny hendley
my baby came from out of nowhere

value	rarity	quality
$$$	♦♦♦♦	★★★

sideshow feat: arthur ponder
sexy lady

value	rarity	quality
$	♦♦♦	★★★

sonny craver
i'm no fool

value	rarity	quality
$	♦♦	★★★

mickie champion
what good am i

value $$
rarity ♦♦
quality ★★★★

danny williams
all those lies

value $$
rarity ♦♦♦♦
quality ★★★

7 miles per hour band
playing your game

value $$
rarity ♦♦♦♦
quality ★★★★

dusty wilson & the corals
it's going to be a tragedy

value $$$
rarity ♦♦♦
quality ★★★★

briggette koberly
don't love me & leave me

value | rarity | quality
$ | ♦♦♦ | ★★

archie hodge
i really want to see you girl

value | rarity | quality
$$ | ♦♦♦♦ | ★★★

al (alonzo) wilson
love you girl

value | rarity | quality
$$ | ♦♦♦♦ | ★★★

devotions
do do de dop

value | rarity | quality
$$$ | ♦♦♦♦ | ★★★★

natural impulse
she went away

value	rarity	quality
$$$$	◆◆◆◆◆	★★★★★

main change
sunshine is her way

value	rarity	quality
$	◆◆◆	★★

tnj's
she's not ready

value	rarity	quality
$$$	◆◆◆◆	★★★

kell osborne
small things

value	rarity	quality
$$	◆◆◆	★★★

del reys
mama was right

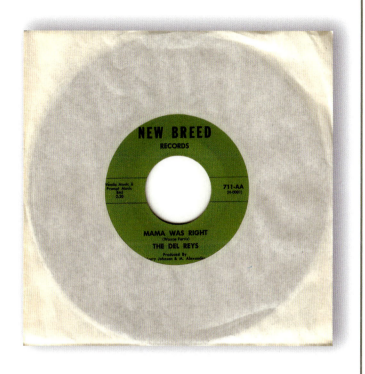

value — $
rarity — ♦♦♦
quality — ★★★

sam dees
in my world

value — $$
rarity — ♦♦♦♦♦
quality — ★★★★★

little reuben
in the name of loneliness

value — $$
rarity — ♦♦♦
quality — ★★★★★

kenny wells
isn't it just a shame

value — $
rarity — ♦♦
quality — ★★★

jades
i'm where it's at

value	rarity	quality
$	♦♦	★★★★

willie wade
when push comes to shove

value	rarity	quality
$	♦♦	★★

jimmie raye
i kept on walkin'

value	rarity	quality
$	♦♦	★★

niteriders
come get these memories

value	rarity	quality
$	♦♦♦	★★

willie tee
please don't go

value: $$
rarity: ♦♦♦
quality: ★★★

marylyn barbarin
just a teenager

value: $$
rarity: ♦♦♦
quality: ★★★

mickey buckins & the new breed
silly girl

value: $
rarity: ♦♦♦
quality: ★★★

cleveland robinson jr
love is a trap

value: $$
rarity: ♦♦♦
quality: ★★★

cleveland robinson
boy

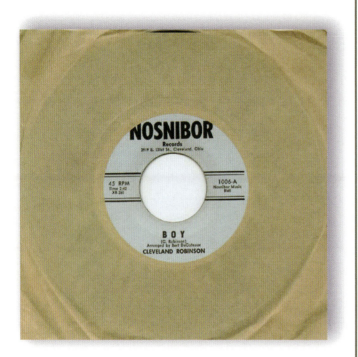

value	rarity	quality
$	♦♦♦	★★

nu-rons
all my life

value	rarity	quality
$$$	♦♦♦♦	★★★

little beaver
i feel my love

value	rarity	quality
$	♦♦♦♦	★★★

barbara jean
while you're out shoppin'

value	rarity	quality
$$	♦♦♦♦	★★★

unknown artist
chairman of the nitty gritty committee

value	rarity	quality
$$	♦♦♦♦♦	★★

sparkels
try love (one more time)

value	rarity	quality
$	♦♦	★★★

jesse johnson
left out

value	rarity	quality
$$	♦♦♦	★★★★

major harris
call me tomorrow

value	rarity	quality
$	♦♦	★★★★

tommy tate
i'm taking on pain

value	rarity	quality
$	♦♦	★★★

sandi sheldon
you're gonna make me love you

value	rarity	quality
$$	♦♦	★★★★★

major lance
you don't want me no more

value	rarity	quality
$	♦	★★★★★

seven souls
i still love you

value	rarity	quality
$	♦	★★★★★

ken williams
come back

value	rarity	quality
$	♦♦	★★★★

johnny robinson
gone but not forgotten

value	rarity	quality
$	♦	★★★★

sandra phillips
i wish i had known

value	rarity	quality
$	♦	★★★★

tan geers
let my heart and soul be free

value	rarity	quality
$	♦	★★★★★

60's Record Company 45 Mailers

icemen
it's time you knew

value	rarity	quality
$$	♦♦♦	★★★★

steinways
my heart's not in it anymore

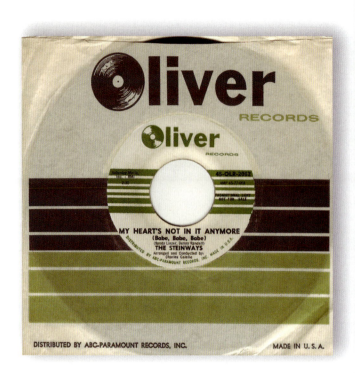

value	rarity	quality
$	♦	★★★★

oracles
i ain't got time

value	rarity	quality
$$$	♦♦♦♦	★★★★

mickey & the soul generation
southern fried funk

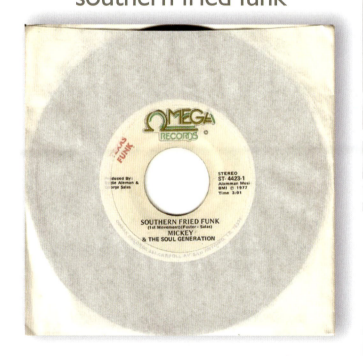

value	rarity	quality
$	♦♦♦	★★★

capitals
i can't deny that i love you

value	rarity	quality
$$$	♦♦♦	★★★★

brice coefield
ain't that right

value	rarity	quality
$	♦♦	★★★★

four-gents
young girls beware

value	rarity	quality
$	♦♦♦	★★★

gwen owens
mystery man

value	rarity	quality
$$	♦♦♦♦	★★★

joe jama
my life

value	rarity	quality
$$	♦♦♦	★★★

fabulous monograms
you are my sweetheart

value	rarity	quality
$$$$$	♦♦♦♦♦	★★★★★

sonny fishback
heart breaking man

value	rarity	quality
$$	♦♦♦♦	★★★

sonny fishback
heart breaking man (alt. version)

value	rarity	quality
$$	♦♦♦♦	★★★★

bobby wisdom
handwriting on the wall

value $$$$$ rarity ♦♦♦♦♦ quality ★★★★

wee
try me

value $$ rarity ♦♦♦♦ quality ★★★

mary saxton
losing control

value $$$ rarity ♦♦♦♦ quality ★★★★★

rita dacosta
don't bring me down

value $ rarity ♦♦♦♦ quality ★★★★

jimmy mack
my world is on fire

value	rarity	quality
$$	♦♦♦	★★★★★

people's choice
savin' my lovin' for you

value	rarity	quality
$	♦♦	★★★

j.t. rhythm
my sweet baby

value	rarity	quality
$$	♦♦♦	★★★★

tommy neal
goin' to a happening

value	rarity	quality
$	♦♦♦	★★★★★

belaires
i got that feelin'

value   rarity   quality

$ ♦♦♦   ★★

al williams
i am nothing

value   rarity   quality

$$$ ♦♦♦♦   ★★★★★

ward burton
sweet temptation

value   rarity   quality

$$$ ♦♦♦♦   ★★★★

daybreak
i need love

value   rarity   quality

$$ ♦♦♦   ★★★★★

admirations
heaven is in your arms

value: $
rarity: ♦♦♦
quality: ★★★

prince paul and the singing imperials
in the beginning (you really loved me)

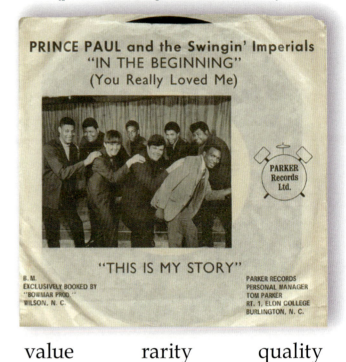

value: $$
rarity: ♦♦♦♦♦
quality: ★★★

hattie winston
pass me by

value: $
rarity: ♦♦♦
quality: ★★★

yvonne baker
you didn't say a word

value: $$
rarity: ♦♦♦
quality: ★★★★★

jerry jackson
it's rough out there

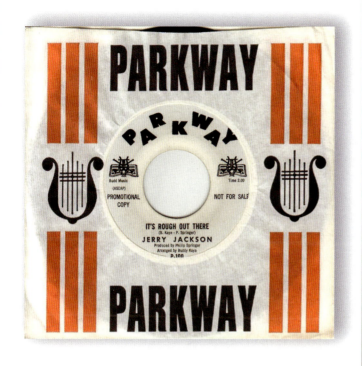

value $
rarity ♦♦♦
quality ★★★★

chubby checker
you just don't know

value $$$
rarity ♦♦♦♦
quality ★★★★★

vickie baines
country girl

value $$$
rarity ♦♦♦♦
quality ★★★★★

christine cooper
heartaches away my boy

value $$
rarity ♦♦♦
quality ★★★★★

bill baker and ork
another sleepless night

value	rarity	quality
$	◆	★★

meridians
he can't dance

value	rarity	quality
$	◆◆	★★

extremes
that's all i want

value	rarity	quality
$	◆◆◆	★★

sherlock holmes
standing at a standstill

value	rarity	quality
$	◆◆	★★★

four perfections
i'm not strong enough

value   rarity   quality
$ ◆   ★★★★★

ad-libs
i don't need no fortune teller

value   rarity   quality
$$ ◆◆◆   ★★★

gerri shivers
let's try it again

value   rarity   quality
$$ ◆◆◆◆   ★★★

naturals
don't just stand there

value   rarity   quality
$ ◆◆   ★★★

tobbi bowe
i can feel him slipping away

value	rarity	quality
$$$	◆◆◆◆◆	★★★★

delvons
girls get ready (here we come)

value	rarity	quality
$	◆◆◆	★★

cheryll ann
i can't let him

value	rarity	quality
$	◆◆◆	★★

admirations
i want to be free

value	rarity	quality
$$$	◆◆◆◆	★★★★

aspirations
you left me

value	rarity	quality
$$$	♦♦♦♦♦	★★★★★

jimmy church
thinking about the good times

value	rarity	quality
$$	♦♦♦♦	★★★★

eddie billups
ask my heart

value	rarity	quality
$$$	♦♦♦♦	★★★★★

georgous george
get up off it

value	rarity	quality
$$	♦♦♦♦	★★★

little eddie taylor
i had a good time

value	rarity	quality
$$	♦♦	★★★★

ambassadors
too much of a good thing

value	rarity	quality
$	♦	★★★★

carol woods and the executives
heart breaker

value	rarity	quality
$	♦♦	★★

sharp-etts
keep looking
(but i guess i'll never find him)

value	rarity	quality
$$	♦♦♦	★★

king moses
i've got this feeling

value	rarity	quality
$$$$	♦♦♦♦♦	★★★★★

nelson sanders
your sweet love

value	rarity	quality
$$	♦♦♦♦	★★

terri goodnight
they didn't know

value	rarity	quality
$$$$	♦♦♦♦♦	★★★★★

jackie day
naughty boy

value	rarity	quality
$$$	♦♦♦	★★★★★

sherri taylor
he's the one who rings my bell

value	rarity	quality
$$	♦♦♦♦	★★★

ernestine eady
let's talk it over

value	rarity	quality
$$$	♦♦♦♦	★★★★

imperials c's
someone tell her

value	rarity	quality
$$$	♦♦♦♦	★★★

stanley evans
we've got a good thing going

value	rarity	quality
$$$$	♦♦♦♦♦	★★★★

melvin brown & james matthews
love stormy weather

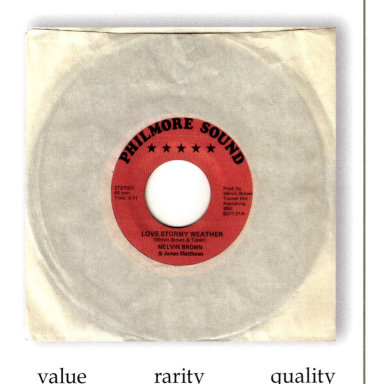

value $$$ rarity ◆◆◆◆ quality ★★★★★

frankie karl
you should'o held on

value $$ rarity ◆◆◆ quality ★★★★

jo ann henderson
baby please don't go

value $$ rarity ◆◆◆◆◆ quality ★★★

lee maye
total disaster

value $ rarity ◆◆◆ quality ★★

earl tobin
she's a killer

value	rarity	quality
$	♦♦♦♦	★★

margaret mandolph
something beautiful

value	rarity	quality
$	♦♦♦	★★★

jackie forrest
the way of love

value	rarity	quality
$	♦♦♦♦	★★★

charles holiday
don't lie

value	rarity	quality
$$$	♦♦♦♦	★★★★

rick hamilton
deeper than the river (this love of mine)

value	rarity	quality
$	♦♦♦♦♦	★★★

marisa gatti
love's what you want

value	rarity	quality
$$	♦♦♦	★★★

william powell
heartache souvenirs

value	rarity	quality
$$$$	♦♦♦♦♦	★★★★★

johnny vanelli
seven days of loving you

value	rarity	quality
$$	♦♦♦	★★★

david thomas
i'll always need you (by my side)

value rarity quality
$$ ♦♦♦♦ ★★

prince ella and sidney jones
baby sugar i love you

value rarity quality
$$ ♦♦♦♦ ★★★

cookie jackson
try love

value rarity quality
$ ♦♦♦ ★★

cookie jackson
do you still love me

value rarity quality
$ ♦♦ ★★★★

sammy lee
what goes around

value rarity quality
$$ ♦♦♦ ★★★

group feat. cecil washington
i don't like to lose

value rarity quality
$$$ ♦♦ ★★★★★

f.j. jones
gone and found another

value rarity quality
$ ♦♦♦♦ ★★

matthew barnett
if your love is real

value rarity quality
$ ♦♦♦ ★★★

in-men ltd
little girl

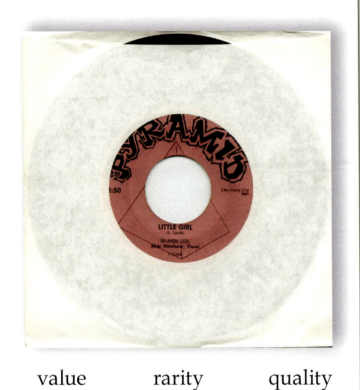

value | rarity | quality
$ | ♦♦♦ | ★★

mac and barb & the gamuts
hold me tighter

value | rarity | quality
$ | ♦♦♦ | ★★

sinceres
don't waste my time

value | rarity | quality
$ | ♦ | ★★★

fortson & scott
sweet lover

value | rarity | quality
$$ | ♦♦♦ | ★★★★

otis lee
hard row to hoe

value: $$
rarity: ♦♦
quality: ★★★

take my heart
mary saxton

value: $$$
rarity: ♦♦♦♦
quality: ★★★

sammy campbell
s.o.s. for love

value: $$
rarity: ♦♦♦
quality: ★★

del-larks
job opening

value: $$$$
rarity: ♦♦♦♦♦
quality: ★★★★★

pinkertones
it's not the way you walk

value   rarity   quality
$$ ♦♦♦♦   ★★★

billy miranda
you could've had a good thing going

value   rarity   quality
$$ ♦♦♦   ★★★

don varner
tear stained face

value   rarity   quality
$$ ♦♦♦   ★★★★★

rufus & roscoe
stay with me

value   rarity   quality
$$ ♦♦♦♦♦   ★★★

fire and fury
i've got what you need

value	rarity	quality
$$	♦♦♦♦	★★★

nelson sanders
i'm so lonely

value	rarity	quality
$$	♦♦♦	★★★★★

ramsey & company
love call

value	rarity	quality
$$	♦♦♦♦	★★★

tavasco
love is trying to get a hold of me

value	rarity	quality
$$	♦♦♦	★★★★

billy sha-rae
pitfall

value: $
rarity: ♦♦♦♦
quality: ★★

magnetics
i have a girl

value: $$$$
rarity: ♦♦♦♦
quality: ★★★★★

future 2000
good things

value: $$
rarity: ♦♦♦♦
quality: ★★★

ron van horn
we've just got to get together again

value: $$
rarity: ♦♦♦♦
quality: ★★

lost soul
a secret of mine

value	rarity	quality
$	♦♦	★★★

lost soul
i'm gonna hurt you

value	rarity	quality
$	♦♦♦	★★★

johnnie hoyle
what about me

value	rarity	quality
$$	♦♦♦	★★★

new wanderers
let me render my service

value	rarity	quality
$$$	♦♦♦♦♦	★★★★★

larom baker
you're the best

value	rarity	quality
$$$$	♦♦♦♦	★★★★

willie feaster & the concrete wall
voices - pt. 1

value	rarity	quality
$$	♦♦♦	★★★

appointments
keep away

value	rarity	quality
$$$	♦♦♦♦	★★★★

dewey black
takin' love where i find it

value	rarity	quality
$$$	♦♦♦♦	★★★

louis curry
you're just plain nice

value	rarity	quality
$$	♦♦♦	★★★

groovettes
think it over baby

value	rarity	quality
$$$	♦♦♦♦	★★★★

sequins
he's a flirt

value	rarity	quality
$$$	♦♦♦♦	★★★★★

carl henderson
i'm scheming

value	rarity	quality
$	♦♦♦	★★

sam cox
life is love

value	rarity	quality
$	♦♦♦	★★★

jesse davis
there's room for me

value	rarity	quality
$$$	♦♦♦♦	★★★★

hayes cotton
black wing's have my angel

value	rarity	quality
$$$	♦♦♦♦	★★★★

billy nitro
as sweet as your love for me

value	rarity	quality
$	♦♦♦♦	★★★

jackey beavers
i need my baby

value	rarity	quality
$$$	♦♦♦	★★★★★

j.j. barnes
our love is in the pocket

value	rarity	quality
$	♦♦	★★★★★

edwin starr
scott's on swingers

value	rarity	quality
$	♦	★★★★★

rose batiste
holding hands

value	rarity	quality
$	♦♦♦	★★★

celest hardie
you're gone

value rarity quality
$ ◆ ★★★

sir ceaser
show me the time

value rarity quality
$$ ◆◆◆◆ ★★★

sammy gaha
thank you, thank you

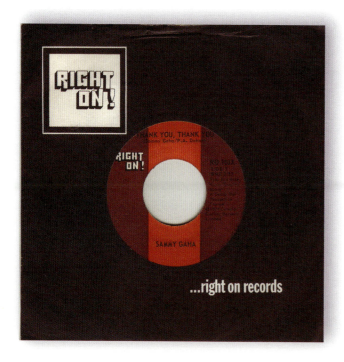

value rarity quality
$ ◆◆◆ ★★

fabulous jades
come on and live

value rarity quality
$$ ◆◆◆ ★★★★

brenda tee
my belief

value	rarity	quality
$$	♦♦♦♦	★★

tempos
lonely one

value	rarity	quality
$	♦♦♦	★★★★

proto jays
you counterfeit girl

value	rarity	quality
$	♦♦♦	★★★★

carroll jones & the soul reflections
hey girl

value	rarity	quality
$	♦♦♦♦♦	★

third guitar
baby don't cry

value	rarity	quality
$	♦♦	★★★★

chuck flamingo
what's my chances

value	rarity	quality
$$$	♦♦♦♦	★★★★

international g.t.o's
i love my baby

value	rarity	quality
$	♦	★★★★★

tolbert
i've got it

value	rarity	quality
$$$	♦♦♦♦	★★★★★

towana & the total destruction
wear your natural, baby

value	rarity	quality
$$	♦♦	★★★★

ty karim
lightin' up

value	rarity	quality
$$	♦♦♦	★★★★★

ty karim
you really made it good to me

value	rarity	quality
$$$	♦♦♦♦	★★★★★

ty karim
you just don't know

value	rarity	quality
$$$	♦♦♦♦♦	★★★★★

bill bush
i'm waiting

value	rarity	quality
$$	♦♦♦	★★★

curtis davis
tell me

value	rarity	quality
$	♦♦♦	★★

storm
can't nobody love me like you do

value	rarity	quality
$$	♦♦♦	★★★

butlers with frank beverly
because of my heart

value	rarity	quality
$$$$	♦♦♦♦♦	★★★★★

victorians
i want to belong to you

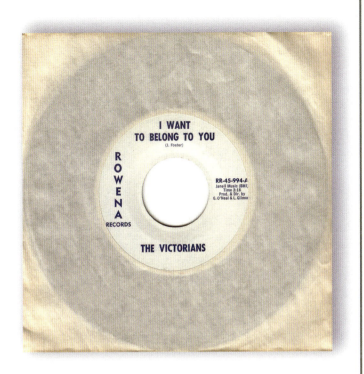

value	rarity	quality
$	♦♦	★★★

caressors
i can't stay away

value	rarity	quality
$$	♦♦♦	★★★★

big ella
the queen

value	rarity	quality
$$	♦♦♦♦♦	★★★

marva lee
old and grey

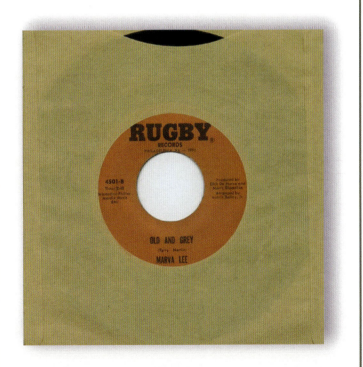

value	rarity	quality
$	♦♦♦	★★★

pearl dowell
good things

value	rarity	quality
$$	♦♦♦	★★★

robert moore
everthing's gonna be all right

value	rarity	quality
$$	♦♦♦	★★★

magnetics
count the days

value	rarity	quality
$$$$	♦♦♦♦♦	★★★★★

magnetics
when i'm with my baby

value	rarity	quality
$$$	♦♦♦♦♦	★★★★★

lee mc kinney & the magnetics
i'll keep holding on

value	rarity	quality
$$$$	◆◆◆◆	★★★★★

eric mercury & the soul searchers
lonely girl

value	rarity	quality
$$$$	◆◆◆◆	★★★★★

mamie p. galore
no right to cry

value	rarity	quality
$$$	◆◆◆◆	★★★★★

apple and the 3 oranges
love brings out the best of you

value	rarity	quality
$$	◆◆◆◆◆	★★★

apple and the 3 oranges
true love will never die

value	rarity	quality
$$	♦♦♦♦	★★★

klas, larry jackson & ricky gaddis
let's make love tonight

value	rarity	quality
$	♦♦♦	★★★

soul brothers inc.
tear drops

value	rarity	quality
$$$$	♦♦♦♦♦	★★★★

red coats revue, inc.
keep on trying

value	rarity	quality
$$	♦♦♦♦	★★★

bobby rich
there's a girl somewhere for me

value: $$$ rarity: ♦♦♦♦ quality: ★★★★

ray raymond & the gaylettes
you say you love me

value: $ rarity: ♦♦♦ quality: ★★

reactions
live my life for myself

value: $ rarity: ♦♦♦ quality: ★★

lenny vestel
its' paradise

value: $$$ rarity: ♦♦♦♦ quality: ★★★★★

curly moore
you don't mean

value	rarity	quality
$$	♦♦	★★★

kylo turner
i'll keep thinking of you

value	rarity	quality
$	♦♦♦	★★

patience valentine
if you don't come

value	rarity	quality
$$	♦♦	★★★

jacki ross
hold me

value	rarity	quality
$	♦♦	★★★

out of sights
for the rest of my life

value	rarity	quality
$$$	♦♦♦♦	★★★★

frank beverly & the butlers
if that's what you wanted

value	rarity	quality
$$	♦♦♦	★★★★★

johhny mc call
let's call it a day

value	rarity	quality
$	♦♦	★★★

johnny maestro
i'm stepping out of the picture

value	rarity	quality
$$	♦♦♦	★★★★★

lord luther
my mistake

value rarity quality
$$ ♦♦♦ ★★★

soulettes
bring your fine self home

value rarity quality
$$$ ♦♦♦♦ ★★★★

answers
thinking of you

value rarity quality
$$$ ♦♦♦♦ ★★★★

tina roberts
one way or the other

value rarity quality
$$$ ♦♦♦♦♦ ★★★★

don gardner
cheatin kind

value   rarity   quality
$$$$ ◆◆◆◆◆   ★★★★★

fabulous play mates
don't turn your back (on loving)

value   rarity   quality
$$ ◆◆◆   ★★★

patrinell staten
little love affair

value   rarity   quality
$$$ ◆◆◆◆◆   ★★★★★

tiara's
loves made a connection

value   rarity   quality
$ ◆◆◆   ★★★

mathew brown
love me just a little

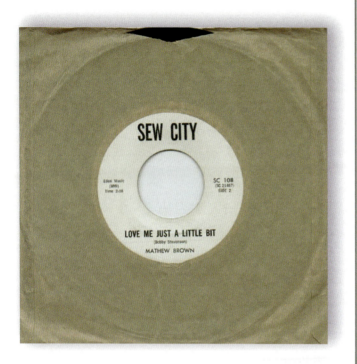

value — $
rarity — ♦♦♦
quality — ★★

flight
playing your games

value — $$
rarity — ♦♦♦♦
quality — ★★★

guitar ray
you're gonna wreck my life

value — $
rarity — ♦♦
quality — ★★★

vickie labat
got to keep hanging on

value — $$
rarity — ♦♦♦
quality — ★★★

senator jones
do you love me

value $$$ rarity ◆◆◆◆◆ quality ★★★

delores ware
strange

value $ rarity ◆◆◆◆ quality ★★

stan martin
big mouth woman

value $ rarity ◆◆◆ quality ★★★

satin
your loves got me

value $$ rarity ◆◆◆◆ quality ★★★

four arts
who do you think you are

value	rarity	quality
$	♦♦♦	★★★

little nicky soul
i wanted to tell you

value	rarity	quality
$$$	♦♦♦♦	★★★★★

condors
let me down easy

value	rarity	quality
$$$	♦♦♦♦♦	★★★

softiques
bash'ful (i'm that kinda girl)

value	rarity	quality
$$$	♦♦♦♦♦	★★★★

fasades
mary sunshine

value | rarity | quality
$ | ♦♦♦♦ | ★★

fred johnson
i feel the soul

value | rarity | quality
$ | ♦♦♦♦ | ★★★

jay walkers
can't live without you

value | rarity | quality
$$ | ♦♦♦♦♦ | ★★★

jessie james
are you gonna leave me

value | rarity | quality
$$$ | ♦♦♦ | ★★★★

ray pollard
this time

value	rarity	quality
$$$	♦♦	★★★★★

cautions
is it right

value	rarity	quality
$$	♦♦♦	★★★

d.c. blossoms
hey boy

value	rarity	quality
$$$	♦♦♦	★★★★

j.d. bryant
i won't be coming back

value	rarity	quality
$$$$$	♦♦♦♦♦	★★★★★

shirley edwards
dream my heart

value	rarity	quality
$$$$	♦♦♦♦	★★★★

cairos
stop overlooking me

value	rarity	quality
$$$$	♦♦♦♦	★★★★★

eddie dave & 4 bars
guess who loves you

value	rarity	quality
$$$	♦♦♦	★★★★

bill dennis
poor little fool

value	rarity	quality
$$$$	♦♦♦♦♦	★★★

les chansonettes
don't let him hurt you

value: $$$
rarity: ♦♦♦
quality: ★★★★

cautions
no other way

value: $$
rarity: ♦♦
quality: ★★★★

prophets
if i had (one gold piece)

value: $$$$$
rarity: ♦♦♦♦♦
quality: ★★★★★

cavaliers
do what i want

value: $$$
rarity: ♦♦♦♦♦
quality: ★★

four sights
love is a hurting game— that i can't win

value — $
rarity — ♦♦
quality — ★★★

johnny praye
can't get too much love

value — $$$
rarity — ♦♦♦♦♦
quality — ★★★★

ted wilson
i can't take no more

value — $$$$
rarity — ♦♦♦♦♦
quality — ★★★★

conquistadores
sadness and madness

value — $
rarity — ♦♦
quality — ★★★

gene toones
what more do you want

value	rarity	quality
$$$$	♦♦♦♦	★★★★★

sandy wynns
i'll give that to you

value	rarity	quality
$	♦♦♦♦♦	★★★

merv murphy
it's growing

value	rarity	quality
$$$	♦♦♦♦	★★★

jokers
soul sound

value	rarity	quality
$$$	♦♦♦♦♦	★★★

timothy wilson
i must love you

value: $
rarity: ♦♦
quality: ★★★★

melvin moore
all of a sudden

value: $$
rarity: ♦♦♦
quality: ★★★★★

leon peterson
now you're on your own

value: $$$
rarity: ♦♦♦♦♦
quality: ★★★★

sammy
i never found a girl

value: $
rarity: ♦♦♦♦
quality: ★★★

norris vines and the luvlines
give in

value	rarity	quality
$$$	♦♦♦♦	★★★★

george blackwell
can't lose my head

value	rarity	quality
$$	♦♦	★★★★★

papabear and the cubs
you're so fine

value	rarity	quality
$	♦	★★

liberation
love looks good on you

value	rarity	quality
$	♦♦♦	★★★

jesse fisher
honey

value	rarity	quality
$$	♦♦♦♦	★★★★

marilyn smith
covers mother

value	rarity	quality
$	♦♦♦♦♦	★★★

pat lewis
no one to love

value	rarity	quality
$$$	♦♦♦	★★★★★

debonairs
loving you takes all my time

value	rarity	quality
$$	♦♦♦	★★★★

richard lackey
the greatest gift

value: $
rarity: ♦♦♦♦
quality: ★★

yvonne vernee
just like you did me

value: $$$$
rarity: ♦♦♦♦
quality: ★★★★★

smokey 007 and the exciters
i'm sorry, please accept my apologies

value: $$
rarity: ♦♦♦♦♦
quality: ★★★★★

frank wilson
do i love you (indeed i do)

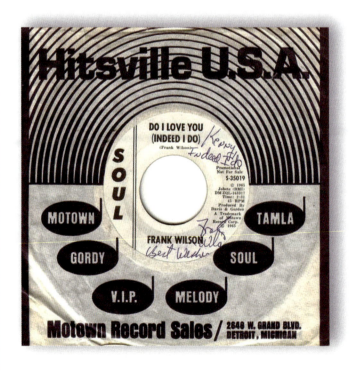

value: $$$$$
rarity: ♦♦♦♦♦
quality: ★★★★★

troy johnson
i want you

value $$ rarity ◆◆◆◆ quality ★★★★

the passionetts
i'm not in love with you anymore

value $$ rarity ◆◆◆◆ quality ★★★

debonairs
please come back baby

value $ rarity ◆◆ quality ★★★

james dockery
my faith in you is all gone

value $$ rarity ◆◆◆ quality ★★★★

smith brothers
there can be a better way

value $$
rarity ♦♦♦♦
quality ★★★★

willie pickett
on the stage of life

value $$
rarity ♦♦♦
quality ★★★★

young brothers
what's your game

value $$$$
rarity ♦♦♦♦♦
quality ★★★★★

judy stokes
kiss our love goodbye

value $
rarity ♦♦♦♦
quality ★★★

ray agee
i'm losing again

value	rarity	quality
$$$$	♦♦♦♦	★★★★★

sweets
something about my baby

value	rarity	quality
$$	♦♦♦♦	★★★★

masquaders
that's the same thing

value	rarity	quality
$	♦	★★★★★

maurice jackson
its to late baby

value	rarity	quality
$$$	♦♦♦♦♦	★★★

dave hall
look at me

value	rarity	quality
$	♦♦♦	★★★

sharpets
lost in the world of a dream

value	rarity	quality
$	♦♦♦	★★★

george hobson
let it be real

value	rarity	quality
$$$	♦♦♦♦	★★★★★

doni burdick
bari track

value	rarity	quality
$$	♦	★★★★★

little tommy
baby can't you see

value — $$
rarity — ♦♦♦
quality — ★★★★

sheepherders
if ever you need me

value — $$$
rarity — ♦♦♦♦♦
quality — ★★★

dickie wonder
nobody knows

value — $$
rarity — ♦♦♦
quality — ★★★★

al johnson
love waits for no man

value — $
rarity — ♦♦♦♦
quality — ★★★

hy-tones
you don't even know my name

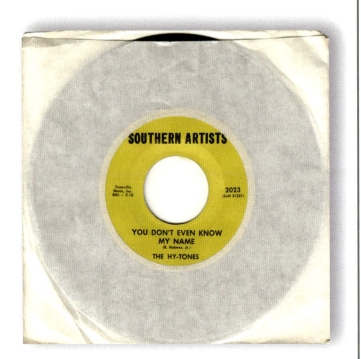

value   rarity   quality
$ ♦♦♦   ★★★

jimmy elledge
sad town

value   rarity   quality
$ ♦♦♦   ★★★

herbert hunter
i was born to love you

value   rarity   quality
$ ♦♦♦   ★★★★★

bernard smith
never gonna let you go

value   rarity   quality
$ ♦♦♦   ★★★

joan dovalle
let me go

value	rarity	quality
$$	♦♦♦♦	★★★

abstract reality
love burns like a fire inside

value	rarity	quality
$	♦♦♦	★★★

appreciations
it's better to cry

value	rarity	quality
$$	♦♦♦	★★★★★

gloria lane
lets get together

value	rarity	quality
$$	♦♦♦♦♦	★★★

sam butler
i can't get over (loving you)

value	rarity	quality
$	♦♦♦	★★★★

little richie
just another heartache

value	rarity	quality
$$	♦♦♦	★★★★★

sonny craver
i wanna thank you

value	rarity	quality
$	♦♦♦♦♦	★★★

mr lucky
born to love you

value	rarity	quality
$$$$	♦♦♦♦♦	★★★★★

gail nevels
taking my mind off love

value: $$$
rarity: ◆◆◆◆◆
quality: ★★★★

del-tours
sweet and lovely

value: $$$$
rarity: ◆◆◆◆◆
quality: ★★★★★

brenda holloway
stay in school

value: $
rarity: ◆◆◆◆◆
quality: ★★★

yvonne daniels
i don't wanna get away from your love

value: $$$
rarity: ◆◆◆◆
quality: ★★★

johnny sayles
i can't get enough

value	rarity	quality
$	♦♦♦♦♦	★★★★★

thomas bailey & the flintstone's band
i need you (most of all)

value	rarity	quality
$$$	♦♦♦♦♦	★★★★★

herman lewis
who's kissing you tonight

value	rarity	quality
$$$	♦♦♦♦	★★★★★

carol frederick
i couldn't care less

value	rarity	quality
$$	♦♦♦	★★★

deadbeats
no second chance

value	rarity	quality
$$	♦♦♦	★★★

billy prophet
what can i do

value	rarity	quality
$	♦♦♦	★★★★★

johnny darrow
love is a nightmare

value	rarity	quality
$	♦♦♦	★★★

minnie jones
shadow of a memory

value	rarity	quality
$$	♦♦♦	★★★

lou pride with bobby gamble
your love is fading

value	rarity	quality
$$$	◆◆◆◆	★★★★

lou pride
your loving is fading

value	rarity	quality
$$$	◆◆◆◆	★★★★

lou pride
i'm com'un home in the morn'un

value	rarity	quality
$$$	◆◆◆◆	★★★★★

alex brown
i'm not responsible

value	rarity	quality
$$	◆◆◆◆	★★★★

pentagons
gonna wait for you

value rarity quality
$$ ♦♦♦ ★★★

harris and orr
spread love

value rarity quality
$$ ♦♦♦ ★★★

pages
heartaches and pain

value rarity quality
$ ♦♦ ★★★★

sex
it's you (baby it's you)

value rarity quality
$$ ♦♦♦♦ ★★★★

headliners
little sister

value	rarity	quality
$	♦♦♦	★★★

true image
i'm not over you

value	rarity	quality
$$	♦♦♦♦	★★★

eula cooper
let our love grow higher

value	rarity	quality
$	♦♦	★★★★★

billy woods
let me make you happy

value	rarity	quality
$$$	♦♦♦♦	★★★★★

perfections
am i gonna lose you

value	rarity	quality
$	♦♦	★★★★

tony troutman
one way love
(ain't no good for two)

value	rarity	quality
$$	♦♦♦♦♦	★★★★

tony galla
in love

value	rarity	quality
$	♦	★★★

herman hitson
you can't keep a good man down

value	rarity	quality
$$	♦♦♦	★★★★

billy wells
this heart these hands

value	rarity	quality
$	♦♦♦	★★★

anetta archibald & chuck tillman combo
clip my wings

value	rarity	quality
$$	♦♦♦	★★★

construction
hey little way out girl

value	rarity	quality
$	♦♦♦	★★★

new yorkers
don't want to be your fool

value	rarity	quality
$	♦♦♦	★★★

ruby sherry
please don't go

value	rarity	quality
$	♦♦	★★★

king sound interpreters and the tips
hi note

value	rarity	quality
$	♦♦♦	★★

barrett strong
let's rock

value	rarity	quality
$$$	♦♦♦♦♦	★

kim weston
a little more love

value	rarity	quality
$$$	♦♦♦♦♦	★★★

calvin williams
lets dance

value	rarity	quality
$$	♦♦♦♦	★★

brooks bros
lookin' for a woman

value	rarity	quality
$$$	♦♦♦♦	★★★★★

lillie bryant
meet me halfway

value	rarity	quality
$$$	♦♦♦♦	★★★★★

master four
love has taken wings

value	rarity	quality
$$$	♦♦♦♦♦	★★★

rocky gil and the bishops
it's not the end

value	rarity	quality
$$	♦♦♦	★★★

trey j's
i found it all in you

value	rarity	quality
$	♦♦	★★★

enchanters
there's a look about you

value	rarity	quality
$$	♦♦♦	★★★

earle's
everybody's got somebody

value	rarity	quality
$$$	♦♦♦♦	★★★★

b.j.b
i gotta make you believe in me

value	rarity	quality
$	♦♦♦	★★

marry clayton
the doorbell rings

value	rarity	quality
$$	♦♦♦♦	★★

james lately
love friends and money

value	rarity	quality
$$$	♦♦♦♦	★★★★★

toni
try my love

value	rarity	quality
$	♦♦	★★★

groovers
i'm a bashful guy

value	rarity	quality
$	◆◆◆◆	★★★

soul shakers
you're turnin

value	rarity	quality
$$	◆◆◆◆	★★★

leonard jewell
bettin' on love

value	rarity	quality
$$$$	◆◆◆◆◆	★★★★★

jimmy gresham
this feelin' i have

value	rarity	quality
$$$	◆◆◆◆	★★★

penetrations
champagne

value	rarity	quality
$$	♦♦♦	★★★

martha star
love is the only solution

value	rarity	quality
$$	♦♦	★★★

ann perry
that's the way he is

value	rarity	quality
$	♦♦♦	★★★★

clifford binns
it was only yesterday

value	rarity	quality
$	♦♦♦♦♦	★★

sterlings
hey boy

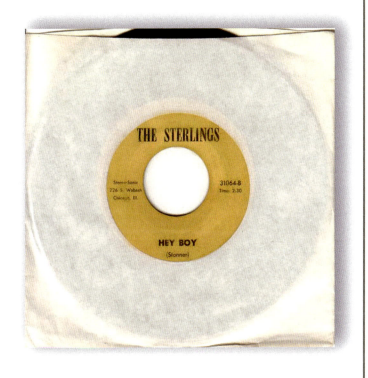

value   rarity   quality
$ ♦♦♦♦   ★★

executive jam
i'm into your love

value   rarity   quality
$$ ♦♦♦♦   ★★★

fantasions
g.i. joe, we love you

value   rarity   quality
$$ ♦♦♦♦   ★★

jay bee and the mighty sensations
praying for an answer

value   rarity   quality
$ ♦♦♦♦   ★★

john and the wierdest
can't get over these memories

value	rarity	quality
$$$	♦♦♦	★★★★★

lewis clark and the explorers
i need your lovin' so bad

value	rarity	quality
$	♦♦♦	★★★

grand prixs
roar of the crowd

value	rarity	quality
$$	♦♦♦♦	★★★

pamela beaty
talking eyes

value	rarity	quality
$$	♦♦♦♦	★★★

tony sams
a thousand miles apart

value	rarity	quality
$	♦♦♦	★★

counts
what's it all about

value	rarity	quality
$	♦♦♦	★★★

john simeone
who do you love

value	rarity	quality
$	♦♦♦	★★★

jimmie & the entertainers
new girl

value	rarity	quality
$$	♦♦♦♦	★★★

sam fletcher
i'd think it over

value — $
rarity — ◆
quality — ★★★★★

rokk
patience

value — $$
rarity — ◆◆◆
quality — ★★★

saxie russell
psychedelic soul - part 1

value — $
rarity — ◆◆◆◆
quality — ★★★★★

la chords
hammer of my heart

value — $
rarity — ◆◆◆◆
quality — ★★

tropics
hey you little girl

value — $
rarity — ♦♦♦
quality — ★★★

dynamics
yes i love you baby

value — $
rarity — ♦♦♦
quality — ★★★★★

sam williams
love slipped through my fingers

value — $$
rarity — ♦♦♦
quality — ★★★★★

herb johnson
i'm so glad

value — $
rarity — ♦♦♦
quality — ★★★★

richard cook
somebody got'a help me

value: $
rarity: ◆◆◆◆
quality: ★★

bill wright
you got a spell on me

value: $
rarity: ◆◆◆◆
quality: ★★

nightchill
hop skip and jump

value: $
rarity: ◆◆◆
quality: ★★

betti lou & bobby adams
dr. truelove

value: $$
rarity: ◆◆◆
quality: ★★★

ogletree brothers
gonna keep a check on you

value $
rarity ◆◆◆
quality ★★★

side show
lonely girl

value $
rarity ◆◆
quality ★★★★

johnny honeycutt
i'm coming over

value $$$$
rarity ◆◆◆◆◆
quality ★★★★

ed crook
that's alright

value $
rarity ◆◆◆◆
quality ★★★

premiers
if your love was true

value	rarity	quality
$	♦♦♦♦	★★

phonetics
just a boy's dream

value	rarity	quality
$$$	♦♦♦♦	★★★★★

royal robins
something about you sends me

value	rarity	quality
$$$	♦♦♦♦	★★★★

ramblers
so sad

value	rarity	quality
$	♦♦♦	★★

east coast rivieras
carolina lady

value	rarity	quality
$	♦♦♦♦	★★

little joe roman
when you're lonesome (come on home)

value	rarity	quality
$$	♦♦♦	★★★★★

clara hardy
i dream of you

value	rarity	quality
$	♦♦	★★★

broken hearted
barbara hall

value	rarity	quality
$$	♦♦♦♦♦	★★★★★

nate evans
main squeeze

value	rarity	quality
$	♦♦♦	★★★

joann courcy
i got the power

value	rarity	quality
$$$	♦♦♦	★★★★

al mc carther
his true love for you

value	rarity	quality
$$	♦♦♦	★★★★★

little joe cook
i'm falling in love with you baby

value	rarity	quality
$	♦♦♦	★★★★

kim katrell
did you see her last night

value rarity quality
$$ ◆◆◆◆◆   ★★★

skytons
my baby is coming home

value rarity quality
$$$$ ◆◆◆◆◆   ★★★★

frankie zhivago young
somebody stole my love

value rarity quality
$$ ◆◆◆   ★★★

limelights
don't leave me baby

value rarity quality
$$$ ◆◆◆◆◆   ★★★★

chashers
without my girl

value	rarity	quality
$$	♦♦♦♦	★★★

sophisticates
i really hope you do

value	rarity	quality
$$	♦♦♦♦	★★★

mixed feelings
sha-la-la

value	rarity	quality
$$$	♦♦♦♦♦	★★★★

shaddows
together again

value	rarity	quality
$	♦♦♦	★★★

candi staton
now you've got the upper hand

value	rarity	quality
$$	♦♦♦	★★★★

ralph graham
she just sits there

value	rarity	quality
$$$	♦♦♦	★★★★

charles mintz
running back

value	rarity	quality
$$$	♦♦♦♦	★★★★

delegates of soul
i'll come running back

value	rarity	quality
$	♦	★★★★

richard caiton
i like to get near you

value	rarity	quality
$$	♦♦♦	★★★★

frank furter & his hot dogs
the green weenie

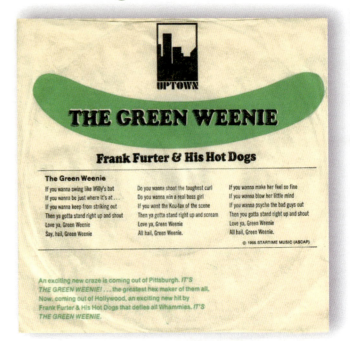

value	rarity	quality
$	♦♦♦♦	★★

intensions
you say that you love me

value	rarity	quality
$$$	♦♦♦♦♦	★★★

toby lark
lots of heart

value	rarity	quality
$$$	♦♦♦♦	★★★

howard tate
you're looking good

value	rarity	quality
$	♦♦♦	★★★★

sonny herman
what about me

value	rarity	quality
$$	♦♦♦♦	★★★★

joe valentine
i lost the only love i had

value	rarity	quality
$$	♦♦♦	★★★

frank dell
he broke your game wide open

value	rarity	quality
$$	♦♦♦♦	★★★★

survivors
good baby

value	rarity	quality
$$	♦♦♦♦	★★

little stanley
out of sight loving

value	rarity	quality
$$$	♦♦♦♦	★★★

little stanley
the stran

value	rarity	quality
$$	♦♦♦	★★

timothy wilson
hey girl, do you love me?

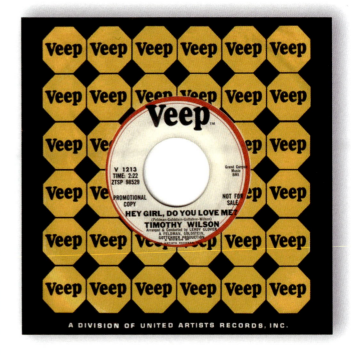

value	rarity	quality
$	♦♦♦♦	★★★

gwen owens
just say you're wanted (and needed)

value	rarity	quality
$$$$	◆◆◆◆◆	★★★★★

two plus two
im sure

value	rarity	quality
$$$$	◆◆◆◆◆	★★★★★

little willie johnson
darling, let's love

value	rarity	quality
$$$$	◆◆◆◆◆	★★★★★

dynells
call on me

value	rarity	quality
$$	◆◆◆	★★★

fred bridges
baby don't weep

value	rarity	quality
$	♦♦♦♦	★★★

kittens
wait a minute (you're getting careless with my heart)

value	rarity	quality
$	♦♦♦	★★★

voices
baby you're messing up my mind

value	rarity	quality
$$	♦♦♦	★★★

carpets
i just can't win

value	rarity	quality
$$$	♦♦♦♦	★★★★

patrice holloway
(he is) the boy of my dreams

value	rarity	quality
$$$$	◆◆◆◆◆	★

andantes
(like a) nightmare

value	rarity	quality
$$$$$	◆◆◆◆◆	★★★

downbeats
put yourself in my place

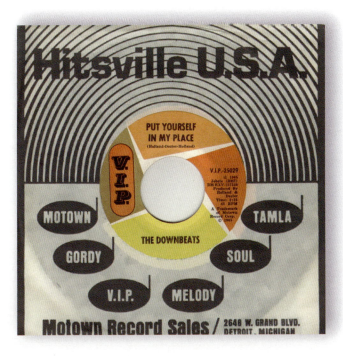

value	rarity	quality
$	◆◆◆◆	★★★

debbie dean
why am i lovin' you

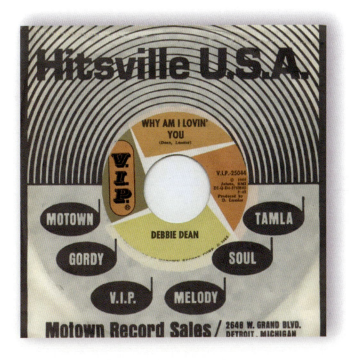

value	rarity	quality
$	◆◆◆	★★★

marilyn barbarin
make it alone

value	rarity	quality
$$	♦♦♦	★★★

robert sanders
what i don't see can't hurt me

value	rarity	quality
$	♦♦♦	★★★

four voices
your love is getting stronger

value	rarity	quality
$$$	♦♦♦	★★★★★

tomangoes
i really love you

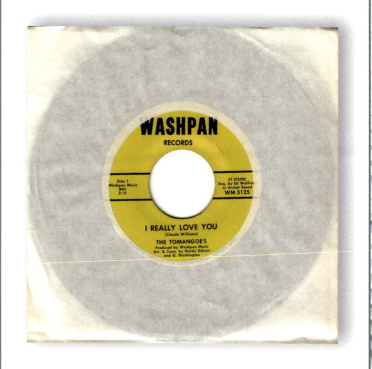

value	rarity	quality
$$$	♦♦♦	★★★★★

bobby bennett
alone with my tears

value	rarity	quality
$$	♦♦♦	★★★

springers
nothing's too good for my baby

value	rarity	quality
$$$$	♦♦♦♦♦	★★★★★

earl harrison
humphrey stomp

value	rarity	quality
$	♦♦♦♦♦	★★

ed bruce
i'm gonna have a party

value	rarity	quality
$$	♦♦	★★★

charts
livin' the nightlife

value: $
rarity: ♦♦♦
quality: ★★★

nella dodds
honey boy

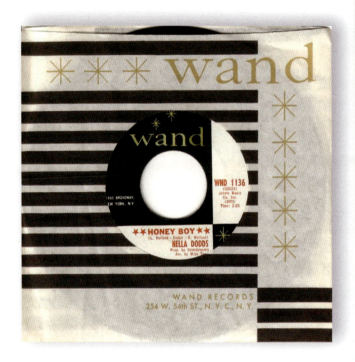

value: $$
rarity: ♦♦♦
quality: ★★★

walter wilson
love keeps me crying

value: $$$$
rarity: ♦♦♦♦♦
quality: ★★★★

gentleman four
you can't keep a good man down

value: $$$
rarity: ♦♦♦♦
quality: ★★★★

billy hines
ling ting tong

value | rarity | quality
$$$ | ◆◆◆◆◆ | ★★

melvin davis
find a quiet place (and be lonely)

value | rarity | quality
$$$ | ◆◆◆ | ★★★★

dobie gray
what a way to go

value | rarity | quality
$$ | ◆◆◆◆ | ★★★

freddie butler
save your love for me

value | rarity | quality
$$$$ | ◆◆◆◆ | ★★★★

steve mancha
did my baby call

value   rarity   quality
$$ ♦♦   ★★★★

conny van dyke
don't do nothing i wouldn't do

value   rarity   quality
$$ ♦♦♦   ★★★★

thee midnighters
you're gonna make me cry

value   rarity   quality
$$$ ♦♦♦♦   ★★★

rosey jones & the superiors
all i need is half a chance

value   rarity   quality
$ ♦♦♦   ★★★

saints
i'll let you slide

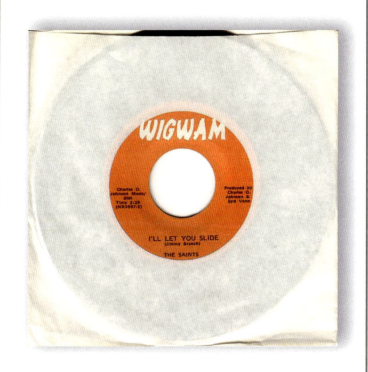

value	rarity	quality
$$$$	◆◆◆◆◆	★★★★

lil major williams
girl don't leave me

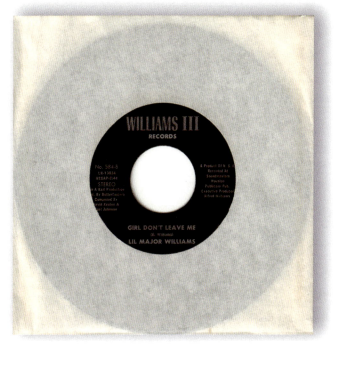

value	rarity	quality
$$$	◆◆◆◆	★★★★★

esther grant
lets get the most out of love

value	rarity	quality
$$$$	◆◆◆◆◆	★★★★

servicemen
are you angry

value	rarity	quality
$$	◆◆◆	★★★★★

royale vii
it's an explosion

value	rarity	quality
$$$	♦♦♦♦♦	★★★

salvadors
stick by me, baby

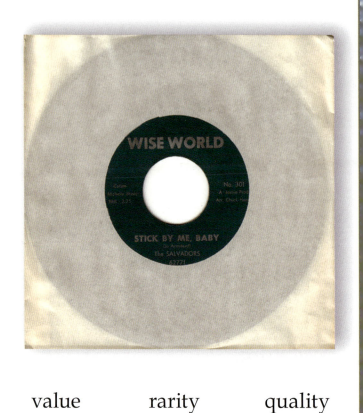

value	rarity	quality
$$$	♦♦♦♦	★★★★★

classics
so glad that i found you

value	rarity	quality
$$$$	♦♦♦♦♦	★★★★★

counts
stronger than ever

value	rarity	quality
$	♦♦	★★

johnny summers
i'm still yours

value	rarity	quality
$$	♦♦♦	★★★★

johnny summers
i can't let go

value	rarity	quality
$	♦♦	★★★★

gary dean
you can say

value	rarity	quality
$	♦♦♦	★★★

lynn vernado
second hand love

value	rarity	quality
$$$	♦♦♦♦	★★★★

Notes